CW00762596

START
OF THE RACE

Studies in Genesis

R.E. Harlow

EVERYDAY PUBLICATIONS INC.
310 Killaly Street W.
Port Colborne, ON L3K 6A6
Canada

HOW TO READ THIS BOOK

The best way to read the Bible is to read a little every day. You can read through the book of Genesis and do this study about Genesis in six months, if you follow the plan on pages 3 and 4.

First, you read a few verses in Genesis, and then you read the paragraph which explains them. You will see on the next page which verses to read every day. On the first day of the month read Genesis 1.1-5. On page 7 you will see a little **1/1** at the left. This shows you where you start reading in this book on the first day. On the second day read Genesis 1.6-13 and read on page 8 what is said about these verses beginning at **1/2**.

This plan will help you to read through the book of Genesis and this book in six months. You can start any month. Write in the name of the month at the top of page 3. If you want to start before the first day of the month, read a little every day, then start over again on the first day of the month. If the month has already started, you could read every day the verses for two days until you catch up.

Some days you will see a question marked with square brackets. You will find the answer for these questions in the Bible in the verses given.

Some days there are no verses to read but questions to answer. There are questions after each chapter of the book on Genesis; these are to help you test yourself. You should answer these questions and then look up the answers on pages 113-117. We hope that you will understand everything and that the Lord will give you blessing and real joy as you read it.

READ THE BIBLE EVERY DAY

DAY	FIRST MONTH	SECOND MONTH	THIRD MONTH
1	1. 1- 5	9.20-29	20. 1- 7
2	1. 6-13	10. 1-14	20. 8-13
3	1.14-19	10.15-32	20.14-18
4	1.20-25	11. 1- 9	21. 1- 7
5	1.26-2.3	11.10-26	21. 8-14
6	2. 4- 9	11.27-32	21.15-24
7	2.10-17	12. 1- 3	21.25-34
8	2.18-24	12. 4-10	22. 1- 8
9	3. 1- 7	12.11-20	22. 9-14
10	3. 8-12	13. 1- 7	22.15-24
11	3.13-19	13. 8-13	23. 1- 9
12	3.20-24	13.14-18	23.10-20
13	4. 1- 7	14. 1-12	24. 1- 9
14	4. 8-17	14.13-16	24.10-14
15	4.18-22	14.17-24	24.15-21
16	4.23-26	15. 1-11	24.22-33
17	5. 1-11	15.12-21	24.34-44
18	5.12-24	16. 1- 6	24.45-61
19	5.25-32	16. 7-16	24.62-67
20	6. 1- 7	17. 1- 8	25. 1- 6
21	6. 8-16	17. 9-14	25. 7-11
22	6.17-22	17.15-27	25.12-18
23	7. 1-10	18. 1- 8	25.19-26
24	7.11-16	18. 9-15	25.27-34
25	7.17-24	18.16-22	26. 1- 5
26	8. 1- 5	18.23-33	26. 6-11
27	8. 6-12	19. 1-11	26.12-16
28	8.13-22	19.12-23	26.17-25
29	9. 1- 7	19.24-30	26.26-35
30	9. 8-19	19.31-38	27. 1- 4

READ THE BIBLE EVERY DAY

DAY	FOURTH MONTH	FIFTH MONTH	SIXTH MONTH
1	27. 5-17	35. 1- 8	42.18-28
2	27.18-29	35. 9-15	42.29-38
3	27.30-40	35.16-22	43. 1-10
4	27.41-46	35.23-29	43.11-15
5	28. 1- 9	36. 1-18	43.16-25
6	28.10-15	36.19-30	43.26-34
7	28.16-22	36.31-43	44. 1- 5
8	29. 1- 8	37. 1- 4	44. 6-13
9	29. 9-20	37. 5-11	44.14-17
10	29.21-30	37.12-22	44.18-34
11	29.31-35	37.23-28	45. 1- 3
12	30. 1- 8	37.29-36	45. 4-15
13	30. 9-24	38. 1-11	45.16-28
14	30.25-36	38.12-19	46. 1- 7
15	30.37-43	38.20-26	46. 8-27
16	31. 1-13	38.27-30	46.28-34
17	31.14-24	39. 1- 6	47. 1- 6
18	31.25-35	39. 7-18	47. 7-12
19	31.36-42	39.19-23	47.13-17
20	31.43-55	40. 1- 8	47.18-31
21	32. 1- 8	40. 9-15	48. 1- 7
22	32. 9-21	40.16-23	48. 8-16
23	32.22-32	41. 1- 8	48.17-22
24	33. 1-11	41. 9-13	49. 1- 7
25	33.12-20	41.14-24	49. 8-12
26	34. 1- 7	41.25-36	49.13-21
27	34. 8-10	41.37-45	49.22-27
28	34.11-17	41.46-57	49.28-33
29	34.18-24	42. 1- 5	50. 1-14
30	34.25-31	42. 6-17	50.15-26

GENESIS

Page

- 1 -
GOD MADE EVERYTHING
chapters 1, 2

1/1 Men have always wondered where they came from. This is because they did not know or did not believe what God says in Genesis 1. The first chapter of the Bible tells that God created the world, animals and man. It is not possible to understand the world around us unless we know where it came from.

It is very wrong to turn away from what God has said. God said that we should read His Word and obey what He says, Revelation 1.3; 22.19. Some people try to add to God's Word and others take away parts of the Scripture. God will judge them, but He will bless those who obey His Word.

Writers of the Bible do not try to prove that there is a God. The first verse simply states that in the beginning *God* created the heavens and the earth. This verse teaches us that God existed before the heaven and the earth. Some people say that God is everything and everything is God. But God is separate from the world which He has made and He is greater than the world. We can be sure that whatever God does He does perfectly, Deuteronomy 32.4. *(Right + fair + faithful God)*.

In verse 2, however, we see that the earth was without form and darkness was over the deep sea. The earth was covered with deep water and thick clouds so that light could not get through to it. We learn from Isaiah 45.18 that God did not create the earth this way.

Isaiah also tells us in chapter 14.12-15 that Satan, also called Day Star, fell into sin. Satan is the ruler of this world, John 12.31, and God's judgment on him may have left the earth as it is seen in Genesis 1.2. From these and other verses we understand that God created the earth perfect and some time later judgment fell on it.

This same verse tells us that God began to restore things and bring order again into the world. The word *wind* means spirit. The Spirit of

God was moving on the surface of the water. Then God said, "Let there be light," and there was light on the earth in the daytime. God saw that the light was good. He divided between light and darkness and called them day and night. This was the *first* day.

God took six days to restore order to the earth and create animals and man. No doubt God could have done it in one minute, but instead of that He did a little bit each day. Some people think the word *day* in Genesis 1 may mean a long time and not just a day of 24 hours. It is true that in the Bible *day* is used of a long time, 2 Peter 3.8, but God could create these things quickly or in a minute if He chose to do so.

The word *create* means to make something out of nothing. The Holy Spirit used this word only three times in Genesis 1: God created the heavens and earth, verse 1; God created sea animals and birds, v.21; and He created man, v.27.

1/2 On the *second* day, God divided the water of the clouds from the water of the sea by putting the clear air in between. This air was called the firmament, or vault, or atmosphere, and it prepared the way for the birds of heaven, which God was going to create. [The word heaven is used in three ways in the Bible: the air (the clouds of heaven) Daniel 7.13; outer space (the stars of heaven) 1 Chronicles 27.23; and where God lives (the God of heaven) Genesis 24.7.]

On the *third* day, God raised the mountains and lands above the water. The dry land appeared and the rest of the water was gathered together in the seas. God also saw that this was good and commanded that grass should spring up, and plants bearing seeds, and fruit trees. So God prepared food for the animals and for the man that He would soon create.

1/3 On the *fourth* day the thick clouds broke up and the stars, sun and moon could be seen on earth. No doubt God had created these long before, 1.1. The word *made* in verse 16 does not mean to create but to *establish*. The regular movement of the sun, moon and stars in the sky helps men to know the seasons of the year. God also saw that this was good.

1/4 Now on the *fifth* day the earth was ready for birds and fish. God commanded these to multiply each according to its own nature. On the *sixth* day God created the animals that live on the land.

1/5 Everything was now ready for the greatest of God's earthly creatures. God decided to make man in His own image and likeness, 1.26. God blessed both the man and the woman and He commanded them to multiply according to their nature. He gave them control over the animal world, 1.28.

Man is like God in that he knows the difference between right and wrong. Man also has a three-part nature: body, soul and spirit, 1 Thessalonians 5.23. In this way he is like the one God, who is Father, Son and Holy Spirit. Only the Lord Jesus is the perfect image of God, Colossians 1.15. As we grow more like Christ we will be more like God.

God considered His work of creation each day and saw that it was good. He finished creating man and everything else and saw that it was *very* good. He had completed His work of creating heaven and earth, so He rested from His work on the seventh day. He blessed the seventh day and called it holy, 2.3.

By resting on the Sabbath day, God established the principle of one day of rest out of seven. In the Old Testament the Law demanded that the people of Israel should observe the Sabbath day and keep it holy, Exodus 20.8. In the New Testament believers are not under law, but we set aside the first day of the week to remember the death and resurrection of the Lord Jesus, to worship Him and to serve Him. However, it is wrong to observe special days as a way to be saved, Galatians 4.10,11.

1/6 In Genesis 2 we have another account of the creation of man but here God is also called Jehovah, or the LORD. The name Jehovah is used of God very often in the Old Testament, especially when God in His great love makes a covenant to bless His people.

After God had made the plants and animals He made man. Man was made of the dust of the ground and God breathed into him the breath of life, 2.7. The body of man is made up of the same common things which are found throughout the world. In this way he is like an animal, but the Lord God breathed into him the breath of life. Man's spirit came from God, but animals do not have spirits. Man is greater than any animal and we should never bow down to an animal or worship the image of an animal.

God planted a garden for man to live in. In addition to many fruit trees, God planted two special trees called the tree of life and the tree of the knowledge of good and evil, 2.9.

1/7 A river flowed out of Eden and divided into four streams, 2.10-14. From the Bible we learn that a river will flow from the new temple in a future day and the water of life will flow from the throne of God, Ezekiel 47.1; Revelation 22.1.

The Lord God put Adam in the garden to take care of it. He told him he could eat the fruit of any tree in the garden, but he must not eat of the tree of the knowledge of good and evil. God warned Adam quite plainly: if he ate of this tree he would surely die, 2.15-17.

1/8 You would think that Adam would be very happy in the garden of Eden. However, God knew that it was not good for him to be alone, so He decided to make a partner for him. First God brought all the birds and animals before Adam and let him give each one a name. Then the Lord God caused Adam to fall asleep and out of one of his bones he built a woman to be his wife. Adam knew that the woman was part of his body. In the garden of Eden the man and the woman did not wear clothes but felt no shame about this, 2.18-25.

In chapter 1 we have the story of God creating the world and all things. In chapter 2 the Lord God created man and supplied him with a wife and a home. In John 1.3 and Colossians 1.16 we see that all things were created by the Son of God, our Lord Jesus Christ. So when we worship Jesus Christ and call Him Lord, we are worshiping the great God, the Creator of all things. The Spirit of God also is seen restoring order to the earth after it became "without form", 1.2.

Teaching about the Church is found in the New Testament, but in the Old Testament we find pictures of this truth. For example, in Genesis 2 we have a picture of the Church. Adam was not complete without his wife, and so the Son of God will never be fully complete or satisfied until His Bride, the Church, is with Him in heaven for ever. The Church is like the Bride of Christ, Ephesians 5.25, and we read of the wedding feast of the Lamb, Revelation 19.7-9.

Man was created for the glory and pleasure of the Son of God. The Lord has commanded us to tell other people about His love. If they are saved they will be added to the Church, the Bride of Christ. This brings the Lord Jesus great glory and joy. When the number of believers is complete the Lord, the Bridegroom, will come back to take His Bride home to be with Himself.

From Genesis chapters 1 and 2 we learn that God is different from, and greater than the world which He has created. God existed before anything else came into being, and He created everything according to His own will and in His own time.

✳ God the Creator has a right to tell us what to do and what not to do. He told Adam not to eat the fruit of the tree of the knowledge of good and evil. In the next lesson we shall see what Adam did about this commandment from God.

Now test yourself

1. How can men know where they come from?

2. What was the world like when God first created it?

3. Where is the word *create* found in Genesis 1?

4. In what way is man like God?

5. Each day except one God saw that His work was good. Which day was that?

6. Where can you read about the Church?

Turn to page 113 to check your answers.

[handwritten notes:]

Read Genesis 1 + Bible

(was perfect but then disorder, dark, formless)

vs 1, vs 21, vs 27 — heaven + earth, man, animals + birds

in his image
✱ knows right from wrong
✱ 3-part nature (body, soul + spirit)
God (Trinity = Father, Son, Holy Spirit).

2nd day
6th day — "very good"

New Testament
① Ephesians 5:25 (Church = Bride of Christ)
② Revelation 19:7-9 (wedding feast of Lamb)

- 2 -
ADAM AND EVE
chapters 3, 4

Adam and Eve fell into sin, chapter 3

1/9 We have seen that God created animals and man, but Genesis 1 and
2 do not tell us anything about angels. The Son of God created all
things seen and unseen, Colossians 1.16, including angels. One of these
angels, called Day Star or Satan, wanted to be above the other angels
and equal with God, Isaiah 14.12-15; Ezekiel 28.13-15. We have seen
that Satan's sin may have been the reason why God judged the world in
Genesis 1.2. Since then Satan has always been the enemy of God and of
God's people. He is always trying to take away honor from the Lord
Jesus Christ by leading men into sin.

In Genesis 3 Satan came to Eve as a snake. He was more clever at
deceiving than any other creature. First he simply asked a question about
the love of God, 3.1. He did not tell Eve she should do anything wrong,
nor did he even say that God was unkind.

Even today Satan often puts doubts in our minds and makes
us wonder if God really loves us. Just remember that God gave
His Son to die for your sins. This proves for ever His wonderful
love to each of us.

The woman answered Satan by saying they could eat the fruit of all
the trees except the one in the middle of the garden. Then she made
God's command worse than it really was, 3.3. God had not told them
that they could not *touch* the tree. So we see that the woman told the first
lie recorded in the Bible.

We should never add to the Word of God nor should we take
away from it. Neither should we listen to the voice of Satan. The
Lord Jesus said Satan was a liar and the father of lies, John 8.44.

Satan knew at once that he had already won a victory by deceiving
Eve, so he quickly told the second lie. He plainly said the opposite of

12

what God had said. God said, "You will die," 2.17; Satan said, "You will not die," 3.4. Satan suggested that God did not really love Adam and Eve and did not want them to be like Himself, by knowing good and evil. Did God know evil? It is true that God knows the difference between what is good and what is evil, but He does not know evil in the sense of committing sin Himself. Ⓝ

Adam and Eve already knew the difference between good and evil. God had told them what they should not do. To obey God would be good; to disobey Him would be evil. Now Satan suggested that Eve could be better or wiser and more like God. She could know evil in the sense of committing sin.

① Please our sinful selves
② lusting for sinful things we see
③ Proud of what we have.

In 1 John 2.16 we read of three things in this world which do not come from the Father. Satan tempted the woman on these three lines. Eve thought she would get something for herself, she would eat the fruit. She could see with her eyes that it was beautiful. She believed it would make her wise and she could be proud of this. Satan himself had fallen through pride because he wanted to be greater than the other angels. The woman listened to Satan and broke God's command. She took the fruit of the tree, ate some of it, and gave some to her husband and he also ate, 3.6.

Ⓝ A man and his wife should love one another and do little things to please each other. However, if one wants the other to commit sin, he or she should refuse at once.

woman was deceived.

Adam was not deceived, 1 Timothy 2.14, and so his sin was worse, but both Adam and Eve broke God's command. In this way the terrible thing called sin came into the hearts of our ancestors. What were the results of their act?

man sinned willingly (worse)

Both guilty.

First, their eyes were opened just as Satan had promised them. This, however, did not make them more like God. Instead, they felt shame because they were wearing nothing. They tried to make up for this by sewing leaves together, 3.7.

1/10 Before he fell into sin Adam enjoyed talking with God. This of course was no longer possible after he had sinned. Adam and Eve tried to hide themselves from God, but God called Adam and he had to come, 3.9. God asked him if he had eaten the fruit of the tree of the knowledge of good and evil. Adam was afraid and ashamed and tried to blame his wife for what he had done, 3.12. What he said was true, but Adam was just as guilty as Eve. Worse still, he said, "The woman you gave me." In these words Adam blamed God saying if God had not given this woman to him, he would not have fallen into sin.

The Bible says that the devil accuses God. Here a man joined with Satan in bringing an accusation against God who is both loving and wise. Nothing could be worse.

1/11 The Lord God then called the woman and she said that the serpent had deceived her, 3.13. So God called the serpent and put a curse on him. The serpent and Satan would forever be enemies of the woman and her children. Some day the woman would have a Descendant who would overcome the serpent, 3.14,15. Jesus? Yes.

This Descendant of the woman is the Lord Jesus Christ. Some translations of the Bible say that many of the woman's descendants would strike at Satan, but the old Hebrew and Greek Bibles speak of one man. All men have committed sin and have put themselves into Satan's power. The Lord Jesus is the only one who has never committed sin so He alone could defeat Satan. But He had to die in order to win the victory. So Satan hurt the Lord Jesus, but the Lord Jesus has destroyed the power of Satan.

Before Adam and Eve sinned God had blessed them, 1.28, and He did not remove this blessing. God put a curse on Satan, 3.14, and on the ground, 3.17; but not on Adam and Eve. However the curse of God is on anyone who does not perfectly keep the law. The Lord Jesus took this curse on Himself, and God gives to the believer a blessing instead of the curse, Galatians 3.10-13. It is God's pleasure to change a curse into a blessing, but He does not usually change a blessing into a curse.

God did not put a curse on Adam or Eve but He did have to punish them. Eve would have children, but only with great pain, and her husband would rule over her, 3.16. Adam would have to work hard to get food, and God told him that he would die and his body would return to the dust of the ground, 3.17-19.

1/12 Eve listened to Satan and Adam listened to Eve instead of listening to God. This brought them great sorrow. But even then God gave them a little comfort. He said that the child of the woman would hurt the serpent's head, 3.15. From this Adam knew that his wife would have a child. He called her name Eve because she would be the mother of all living people, 3.20.

God also showed grace in time of judgment, because He supplied coats of skin for Adam and Eve to wear, 3.21. We can be sure that God killed an animal for this, and the dying animal was a picture of the death of our Lord Jesus Christ.

Adam and Eve did not die that very day but they began to die and did die many years later. What is death? When a person dies his spirit leaves his body; it is separated from the body, James 2.26. The Bible also uses the word death when it speaks of a man who is separated from God. We were spiritually dead because of our sins, Ephesians 2.1, but now we have life. God had said that Adam and Eve would die the day they ate the fruit of the tree. They were separated from God; that very day they were spiritually dead.

God drove Adam and Eve out of the garden to keep them from eating the fruit of the second tree, the tree of life, 3.22-24. He put angels at the east side of the garden so Adam and Eve could not return. If they had obeyed God's simple command perhaps God would have led them to the tree of life and given them the fruit to eat so they would have lived for ever. Instead, God has appointed that men must die, Hebrews 9.27. But He has also given His Son that we might live for ever in Him.

So our first ancestors fell into sin by not obeying God's one command. They have passed on to us a sinful nature. Adam, the first sinner, was driven from God, but we can find true joy in God's presence. All Adam's descendants must learn that they are *NB* sinners and are separated from God. We can come back to God *NB* by faith in the Lord Jesus Christ. Adam himself showed that he had faith in God's Word when he called his wife the mother of all living people. God gave Adam and Eve coats of skin and taught them that they could come to Him if they brought a blood sacrifice. "God cannot forgive sin unless blood is shed," Hebrews 9.22.

⤷ *Christ's death on cross.*

Cain and Abel, chapter 4

1/13 Eve too believed the promise of God that she would have a child. A baby boy was born and she called his name Cain, a name which means "received from the Lord." She seemed to think that this child would overcome the snake. Later, Abel was born. When the boys grew up, Abel became a shepherd and Cain became a farmer. They both wanted to bring an offering to the Lord. Abel knew that he was a sinner and that he must die for his sins. He also knew that God had killed an animal for his father and mother. Abel brought a sheep to the Lord, to show that he needed someone to die for him. This showed Abel's faith.

Cain knew these things also, but instead of a sheep he brought something from his garden, which he had produced by his own hard work. Many people since then have followed the way of Cain. They do

not accept God's Word which says they are sinners. They bring their
own works to God for salvation, Titus 3.5, instead of coming in the
name of Christ. Abel brought a better sacrifice than Cain, Hebrews 11.4,
and we can bring a better Sacrifice (the Lord Jesus) than Abel did,
Hebrews 12.24.

God accepted Abel's offering but not Cain's and this made Cain
very angry. What right did Cain have to be angry? God is wiser than
man and Cain should have asked God to show him what was wrong.
God gave him another chance to bring a proper sacrifice. In the Old
Testament, the word *sin* is the same as *sin offering*. Verse 7 could mean
that a sheep was lying at the door and Cain could offer it for his sin if he
wished to do so.

1/14 Instead Cain rose up and killed his brother Abel, 4.8. God called
Cain to account but Cain acted as if he were innocent. Of course it
is not possible to hide anything from God, as we saw in 3.8,9. God put a
curse on Cain, 4.11, but promised to protect his life, 4.15. If any of
Cain's brothers killed him God would punish that man seven times. God
showed grace to Cain, but Cain never repented. He went away from
God, built a city, and named it after his son, 4.16,17.

Think about the way of Cain, Jude 11. Cain refused God's
Word and brought an offering which he had chosen himself.
God did not accept this so Cain became very angry with God.
God gave him another chance, but Cain became so angry and
jealous of his brother that he killed him. We can see how Cain
really felt by the way he answered back to God, 4.9; and by saying that God's punishment was too severe, 4.13. At the end of
all this he went still further away from God.

Cain belonged to the Wicked One, 1 John 3.12. He learned
his lessons well from Satan who was a murderer from the
beginning, John 8.44. However, I am no better if I hate my
brother, 1 John 3.15.

1/15 Cain married one of the daughters of Adam and Eve. Years later
the law said that a man could not marry his own sister,
Deuteronomy 27.22, but in those early days it was different. We read
about Cain's family in 4.18-24. Some of his descendants became great
men in the earth but none of them is said to have had faith in God. One
of them, Lamech, married two wives, 4.19. He followed his ancestor
Cain's example by killing a man, 4.23. Then he tried to take God's
promise to Cain for himself, 4.24.

Today also we see men who live in sin and then try to take one part of God's Word to defend themselves. If they really repent God will forgive them.

1/16 Adam and Eve had many children after Abel died. Seth was born and Eve accepted him as a gift from God in the place of Abel, 4.25,26. The Lord Jesus Christ was born many years later; He was a Descendant of Seth, Luke 3.38. When Seth's son Enos was born men began to call on the name of Jehovah. But we shall see that most men did not obey God's commands.

In chapters 3 and 4 we have seen a great deal of sorrow. There are some verses, however, which make us think of the Lord Jesus Christ. The Descendant of the woman would one day win the victory over Satan but in doing so, He would Himself be hurt, 3.15. The Lord Jesus Christ was put to death on the cross, but He also rose from death. By dying He defeated Satan.

The Lord God made coats from the skin of an animal for Adam and Eve. That animal also makes us think of Christ. By His death, the Lord can supply the clothing of righteousness for all who believe.

But some still try to come to God in the way of Cain; they bring their own good works. However, God will never accept them. We should come and present the Lamb of God; we will never be refused.

Now test yourself

1. Who told the first lie recorded in Scripture? *Eve : "God said don't touch the tree"*

2. In what way did pride lead Eve into sin? *She believed by eating the fruit she would be wise and would be proud of this.*

3. Which words in verse 12 did Adam use to blame his wife for his sin? *"You gave me this woman and she gave me the fruit to eat"*

4. How did God show grace to Adam and Eve? *Clothed them in animal skins & promised Eve's descendant would defeat Satan.*

5. When did Adam die? *He died spiritually when he committed the sin of disobeying God. Gradually died physically from then onwards.*

6. Did God give Cain another chance? *Yes - if he did things well he would accept him. Cain didn't repent. God cursed him but put protection on him.*

Turn to page 113 to check your answers.

Adam + Eve
|
Seth
↓

⋮ Noah.
v
Jesus.

FROM NOAH TO ABRAM
chapters 5 - 11

1/17 *We have seen that God created man and all things. <u>God did</u>*
<u>not create evil but He created beings who could choose between</u>
<u>what is good and what is evil.</u> Unhappily, <u>Eve and Adam chose what was</u>
<u>evil,</u> so God could not allow them to remain near Him because He is
holy. The first parents of the human race <u>passed on to all their descen-</u>
dants a sinful nature. In Lesson 3 we read of Enoch, Noah and his sons,
the flood and the tower of Babel.

Noah's ancestors, chapter 5

In verses 1 and 2 we read again that God created Adam like Himself.
He made both man and woman and blessed them. The Holy Spirit does
not say anything more in this chapter about the sin of Adam. His descendants for 1,556 years are listed in chapter 5. When Adam was 130 years
old, he became the father of a son like himself, whose name was Seth.

 All men are in a way like God. This is one reason why men
should <u>not kill other people,</u> Genesis 9.6.

Adam and Eve had many children and their children all had many
more children. Only ten of their names are given in chapter 5 and these
<u>ten men were all men of faith.</u> This chapter gives the descendants of
Adam down to Noah. These names are found again in 1 Chronicles 1.1-4.
Our Lord Jesus Christ was a descendant of Noah, and these ten names
are seen again in Luke 3.36-38. We shall see that all men, except Noah
and his family were destroyed at the time of the flood. Just as <u>Adam is</u>
<u>the ancestor of all men,</u> so Noah is the ancestor of all men who <u>have</u>
<u>lived since the flood.</u> Therefore, <u>Noah's ancestors are our ancestors.</u>

These ten men all believed God and lived for many years. In chapter
4 we read about the great works of the <u>sons of Cain,</u> but after chapter 4
nothing more is heard of them. They were <u>important to the men of their</u>
<u>own time; that is all.</u> The men of faith in chapter 5 lived long lives for

the glory of God. They were important in God's sight, and this is the greatest thing for any man, to please God.

1/18 God created man and He could let some of them live many years if He wanted to do so. Although we do not see men living nearly so long today we can believe that men lived longer before the flood because the Bible is true. Even so it is said of each one, "and he died."

Only Enoch was different. He was 65 years old when he became the father of Methuselah and after that Enoch walked with God 300 years. He pleased God and was taken up to be with God without dying, 5.24; Hebrews 11.5.

Do not think that it was easy to walk with God or to please God in those days. There were many wicked men in Enoch's time and he prophesied that God would come to judge them, Jude 14,15.

1/19 Enoch called his son Methuselah which means, "when he dies He will send." Enoch was a prophet but he may not have known at first what this name meant. What would God send when the new baby died? Methuselah found out that God was going to send a flood of water on the earth. The flood came the very year that Methuselah died. God in grace held back the judgment so that all men could be warned.

AGE OF METHUSELAH

Methuselah was	187 years old when Lamech was born	5.25
Lamech was	182 years old when Noah was born	5.28,29
Noah was	600 years old when the flood came	7.11
(add these years)		
Methuselah was	969 years old when flood came	

Methuselah died when he was 969 years old, 5.27, the very year the flood came.

Noah was about 500 years old when he had three sons, Shem, Ham and Japheth. This does not mean that they were all born at the same time. Ham was called the youngest son in 9.24, so he was not born at the same time as the others. Actually Noah was 503 years old when Shem was born:

Noah was	600	years old when the flood came,	7.11
Shem was	100	years old when his son was born, This was two years after the flood was over, about three years after it began.	11.10
Shem was	97	years old when flood came.	
Noah was	503	years old when Shem was born.	

The Flood, chapters 6 - 8

1/20 During the 1500 years from Adam to Noah many people were born and the number of men on the earth increased greatly. They all had a sinful nature handed down from Adam and Eve but a few of them trusted in God and did His will.

Satan did not give up his efforts to attack God and to lead men into sin. Wicked spirits helped Satan in this. Who are these wicked spirits? When Satan himself first fell into sin many angels followed him, Revelation 12.9. God judged them also and put some of them into chains, 2 Peter 2.4; Jude 6. Like Satan, the rest of them are able to move around and continue their evil doings. These fallen angels are also called wicked spirits or demons. In the end God will certainly judge them.

We know from the New Testament that wicked spirits try to enter the body of a man and control him; for example see Luke 11.24-26. In Genesis 6.2, the words *sons of God* may mean angels who fell. Angels are called sons of God in Job 38.7. Holy angels in heaven do not marry, Matthew 22.30, but men who allow spirits to control them could of course get married.

This verse (6.2) may also mean that true believers in God began to mix with the world and marry unbelievers; or that men began to follow the example of Lamech, 4.19, and take more than one wife each. Others think that *sons of God* were princes of the nations. None of these explanations tell why their children would be mighty men. The word Nephilim means the *fallen ones*, and is found only in verse 4 and in Numbers 13.33.

One thing is perfectly clear: God was very angry with men. First He said that His Spirit would not always live with men but men might live for 120 years, 6.3. But men still would not change their evil ways.

Then God decided that He would have to destroy both men and animals, 6.5-7. When He had created man He wanted to bless him, but God changed His mind because of man's evil heart.

1/21 The fact that God changed His mind does not mean that God did not know everything from the beginning. He knew quite well what would take place. God had shown grace to men for hundreds of years but men returned all this with more and more sin. Their hearts became so wicked that God had to change His mind. Instead of blessing He had to bring in judgment.

Only Noah was righteous. He gained favor with God and walked with God as Enoch his ancestor had done, 6.8-10.

God saw that the earth was full of evil and He told Noah He would destroy the earth and all men, 6.11-13. He told Noah to make a ship or "ark" out of wood. It was to be about 150 yards (138m) long, 25 yards (23m) wide and 15 yards (14m) high. Both inside and outside Noah was to put a thick black material called pitch to keep the water out. The ark would have three floors or decks, a roof or window, but only one door, 6.14-16.

1/22 God told Noah that He would bring a flood of water on the earth to destroy everything. Noah was told to bring his wife, his sons and their wives, into the ark and they would be saved. He also was to take in two animals of every kind, two birds of every kind and enough food for all, 6.17-22. Noah obeyed God in all these things.

The Lord Jesus spoke about those very days and said that men were eating and drinking and getting married, Matthew 24.38. These things are not wrong or sinful, but men were forgetting about *God*. The Lord taught that it would be the same in the end of this age. Today, many men do not live in great sin but they just live as if there were no God. They will not be prepared for the Lord when He comes.

Noah was building the ark for many years and he was also warning the people at the same time. Noah was a preacher of righteousness, 2 Peter 2.5. No doubt he told the people about Adam's sin, about Cain and Abel, Seth, and Lamech, the descendant of Cain. As the time grew shorter he must have told them about Enoch and Methuselah, Noah's grandfather. When Methuselah died, Noah understood that God was soon going to send a flood of water upon the earth. The ark was big enough to hold hundreds of people but no one believed that God was going to send the flood. Noah told them about God's righteousness and God's love, but without success.

for sacrifice

1/23 At last Jehovah told Noah to go into the ark, 7.1-5. He was to take twelve more of each of the clean animals and birds. (In Leviticus 11 we will learn which animals and birds are clean and which are not clean.)

By now Noah was 600 years old. Eight people in all went into the ark: Noah and his wife, and his three sons and their wives. A week later the flood came, 7.6-10.

1/24 On the 17th day of the second month the rains came down and the waters from below came up. The very day the Lord shut Noah in
1/25 the ark the rain started, 7.11-16. It kept on raining for 40 days and 40 nights. The water got higher and lifted up the ark. The water rose 7½ yards (7 meters) above the highest mountain and all living things were destroyed, except fish. The flood lasted for about five months, 7.17-24.

1/26 Even before the end of five months God thought about Noah and the waters began to go down. The ark came to rest on a mountain on the seventeenth day of the seventh month. The waters kept on going down and on the first day of the tenth month Noah could see the tops of the mountains, 8.1-5.

1/27 Noah sent out an unclean bird after another 40 days, 8.6,7; Leviticus 11.13-15. This bird was satisfied with the world still under God's judgment. It could find enough to eat in the bodies of dead animals and did not return to the ark. So Noah sent out a clean bird which could be used for a sacrifice, 8.8; Leviticus 1.14. The clean bird returned to Noah so he knew that the water still covered the ground. A week later he let the bird go and it came back with a leaf in its mouth. The third time it did not return any more, 8.9-12.

1/28 At last Noah looked out and saw that the ground was dry. Still he waited almost two months more until God told him to go out with his wife, his sons and their wives, and all the animals, 8.13-19.

First Noah built an altar to the Lord and offered a sacrifice of every clean animal and bird. God saw in these sacrifices a picture of His Son who died for all men. God promised that He would never again destroy the world with a flood. As long as the earth remains there will be summer and winter, day and night, 8.20-22.

The ark is a picture of our Lord Jesus Christ who saves us from the storm of God's judgment. We have seen that Noah put material called pitch, inside and outside the ark to keep the water out. The word for *pitch* also means to make atonement, and is translated that way many times, for example, Leviticus 1.4. This makes us think of the work of Christ on the cross which keeps us safe in the day of God's anger.

There was only one door in the ark and Noah's family had to enter by faith. There's also only one Way for us to be safe: Christ is the Way.

Inside the ark Noah and his family were safe and they knew it because of God's Word. God also told Noah to take in enough food for his family and for the animals. So in Christ, God supplies all our needs. Like Noah we ought to tell men that God is angry with their sin but that He saves us completely in Christ.

Noah to Abraham, chapters 9 - 11

1/29 *In chapter 9 we read the story of Noah's life after the flood until he died. In chapter 10 we have the names of the sons of Japheth, Ham and Shem. We will learn about the tower of Babel and the beginning of the history of Abraham in chapter 11.*

After the flood there were only four men and four women in the whole world. God blessed Noah and his sons and told them to have many children. He gave them all living things and said they could eat whatever they wanted, except blood, 9.1-4.

God told them that if any man kills another, other men should put him to death, 9.5-6. In these words God established human government in the earth and this is still God's will for today. The laws of some states do not require that a murderer should be put to death and Christians are told to obey their government, Romans 13.1-7. No ordinary man has the right to put anyone to death.

1/30 Then God made a covenant with Noah and his sons, 9.8-17. He promised them that He would never again destroy all men and animals by a flood. He put a rainbow in the sky as a sign and He will never forget His covenant. The beautiful colors of the rainbow curve across the sky after the rain and also remind us about God's promise.

The world around us seems to be as wicked as it was before the flood. Some day God will destroy it again, not by water but by fire, 2 Peter 3.5-7. Noah was a man of righteousness, Ezekiel 14.14, and we have seen that he was a preacher of righteousness, 2 Peter 2.5. By faith he received the gift of righteousness, Hebrews 11.7. We should follow his example, believe the Word of God and warn men around us.

2/1   However, it is quite possible to obey God's Word and go on with the Lord for many years, then fall into sin before life is over. This is what happened to Noah, 9.20-27. After the flood Noah planted some grapevines, drank too much wine, and became drunk. His son Ham came into the tent and saw him lying without any clothes. Ham told his brothers Shem and Japheth and they came in and covered their father. Noah learned what they had done and blessed Shem and Japheth, but put a curse on Canaan, one of the four sons of Ham.

Noah had fallen into sin, but even so he could speak here as a prophet. God had already blessed Ham, 9.1, and He would not change this. Canaan is the son of Ham, verse 22, and he may have been with his father at that time. The prophecy, however, looks forward to the future. Shem was blessed to be the ancestor of Abraham, of King David, and of the Lord Jesus Christ as a Man. Also many years later God gave the land of Canaan to the descendants of Abraham. In the time of Joshua, the people of Israel defeated the nations of Canaan. Most of those nations came from the sons of Ham, but they too will get a blessing if they come to Shem's Descendant, the Lord Jesus Christ.

Noah died when he was 950 years old. He lived longer than Adam or any other man except Methuselah and Jared. When Noah died Abraham was already 57 years old.

2/2   Chapter 10 gives us another long list of names, the names of the descendants of Japheth, Ham and Shem. These descendants of Japheth lived in lands which later on belonged to the Gentiles, 10.2-5. The descendants of Ham lived in Africa and other countries around Palestine, 10.6-20. One descendant was called Nimrod and he was a mighty hunter before the Lord, 10.8-11. This does not mean that he pleased the Lord. In fact, he began to set up his own kingdom, which included Babel and later became the wicked city of Babylon.

Other descendants of Ham lived in Nineveh, Egypt, Canaan, in the land of the Philistines, and in Sodom and Gomorrah. We will read of all these places later on in the Bible.

2/3   The descendants of Shem are listed in 10.21-31. Why are they important? The main purpose of the Spirit of God is to glorify the Lord Jesus Christ. The Holy Spirit inspired men to write the Old Testament and He led them to speak about Christ. Even this list of names of men who lived and died long ago makes us think about the Lord Jesus. Shem, Arphaxad, Heber and Peleg, 10.21-25, are all ancestors of Abraham. Therefore, they are also ancestors of the Lord Jesus Christ, as a Man, Luke 3.35,36.

Noah walked with God and he is a picture of Christ. The ark is a picture of Christ because He saves us from judgment if we believe. We should look for pictures of Christ on every page of Scripture.

The tower of Babel, chapter 11

2/4 God had commanded Adam and Noah and his sons to spread out and fill the earth with their children, 1.28; 9.1. Instead of that they decided to settle down in the east and to build a city and a tower. They did not want to spread over the whole earth, 11.1-4.

We see here again that men did not obey God's will. God spoiled their plan by mixing up their language so they could not understand one another. This was the beginning of the many languages which are in the world today.

On the day of Pentecost people from many different lands heard the gospel in their own language and understood it, Acts 2. For a short time God changed the judgment which He put on men at the Tower of Babel. Today we must study the language of other people so that we can tell them the gospel of our Lord Jesus Christ.

Babel was later called Babylon and the people of Babylon were always enemies of Israel. In the time of King Nebuchadnezzar, Babylon attacked Jerusalem and destroyed it. The Babylonians carried off the people of Israel as prisoners, 2 Kings 25.1-11. In Revelation 17 and 18 Babylon is a picture of the false church and receives her judgment from God.

2/5 Next we have a list of the descendants of Shem down to the time of Abram, 11.10-26. Before the flood men often lived to be 800 or 900 years old but after the flood the life-span of men was getting shorter. Shem lived to be 600 but Terah died when he was 205, 11.32. These ten men from Shem to Abraham were all ancestors of our Lord Jesus Christ, Luke 3.34-36.

2/6 The book of Genesis from chapter 12 to the end tells us the story of four men: Abraham, Isaac, Jacob and Joseph. Abraham's name at first was Abram, and we read a little about his family in 11.27-32. Abraham's brother Haran died before his father Terah. Sarai, Abraham's wife had no children. Terah took Abraham his son, and Lot his grandson, and their families and left the city of Ur to go to the land of Canaan. They stopped about half way and lived in Haran until Terah died.

In Lesson 4 we will go on to the second part of the book of Genesis, but first let us look back at chapters 1 to 11. It is beautiful to see how the Holy Spirit teaches us the truth in these eleven chapters. The book starts by telling us that God created the heaven and the earth. In six days He renewed and restored the earth. He created man and woman and gave them charge over the animals. God placed Adam and Eve in a garden and told them to take care of it. This suggests that an enemy might try to get in. There was only one thing they were not allowed to do — eat the fruit of the tree of the knowledge of good and evil.

Everything showed the love of God, but Satan persuaded Eve that God was not kind. When Adam and Eve fell into sin they were afraid and ashamed. God had to punish them as well as the serpent, and He drove Adam and Eve from the Garden of Eden. Still God showed His grace by giving them coats of skin and by promising that the Son or Descendant of the woman would overcome the enemy in the end.

Children were born but each child had a sinful nature. Cain murdered his brother, Lamech killed a young man, and soon all men were so evil that God had to destroy His own work. Only Noah found favor before God. Noah built the ark and preached for many years but no one believed him except his own family. So the first part of man's history ends in failure.

In the flood God showed that He hated sin. Only eight people lived and you might think that they had learned their lesson and with a new start all would be well. However, Noah himself soon fell into sin. Men really showed that they did not want to obey God when they built a tower and a city. God judged men for this but He did not destroy them. This time He called out one man, Abraham, and gave him special revelations of Himself. The second part of the book of Genesis tells the story of Abraham and his descendants until the time the nation of Israel was formed.

In these eleven chapters we learn about God's power, His love and His righteousness. We also learn that Satan hates God and man, and that man is weak and sinful. God wants us to know that we need a Savior and that He has given us one, the Lord Jesus Christ.

Now test yourself

1. In what way was Enoch different from the nine other men whose names are in chapter 5? *He walked with God; He did not die but was taken up to heaven by God.* ✓

2. What were Enoch's two prophecies? *...led son Methuselah "When he dies He will Send"; Predicted flood would come in delay/year son died.* ✓

3. How do we know that Noah preached to other men? *2 Peter 2:5 Preacher of righteousness.* ✓

4. Show how Noah and the ark are pictures of Christ. *Ark: keeps us safe when God judges (storm/wrath). Noah: Had to enter Ark through one door (Christ is only way-faith).*

5. Why are the descendants of Shem important? *direct line to Jesus Christ.* ✓

6. Why did God judge men at Babel?

→ They refused to obey God's order to spread over the earth and multiply. Chose to settle & build tower to show their fame/self importance. ✓

② Lord would come to judge wicked men (Jude 14/15) ✓

Turn to page 113 to check your answers.

- 4 -
ABRAM
chapters 12 - 17

2/7 *The story of Abraham is given in chapters 12-24, but in this lesson we will take up only the first part. We will read about how God called him, chapter 12, and then about three other persons who came into Abraham's life: Lot, Melchizedek and Ishmael. In chapter 17 God changed his name from Abram to Abraham.*

The call of Abram, chapter 12

God appeared to Abram while he was still in the city of Ur, before his father moved to Haran, Acts 7.2-4. God told him to leave his country and family and promised to make him into a great nation, Genesis 12.1-3.

2/8 At first Abram obeyed only part of God's command. Both Terah and Lot went with him and he stopped half way, at Haran. When his father Terah died, Abram obeyed the command of the Lord more fully but still he took Lot with him.

Took family too.

It is not good enough to obey only *part* of God's command. Abram wasted many years in Haran before he reached the land of Canaan, and Lot caused him both trouble and sorrow. We can expect God's blessing only if we obey Him fully.

When Abram was 75 years old, his father Terah died and Abram came to the land of Canaan. The Lord appeared to Abram at Moreh and promised to give him the whole land, 12.6,7. Right there Abram built an altar to Jehovah. We will see later that the Lord appeared to Abram again, 17.1; 18.1; and also to Isaac and Jacob, 26.2, 24; 35.9. We know that no man has ever seen God in all His glory, John 1.18, but God's Son has shown Him to us. These verses in the Old Testament say God appeared so we understand that it was God the Son who appeared to these men of faith in Old Testament times.

Abram and Lot kept moving through the land of Canaan toward the south which is called the Negev, 12.8-10. They could not get enough food to eat so they traveled down to Egypt. But God had commanded Abram to live in the land of Canaan, and He did not send him from Ur to die from hunger in Canaan. Abram should have believed that God would look after him and his family.

 God sent this time of hunger to test His servant. We too must learn to trust Him in difficult times.

2/9 Abram was like Adam; he became afraid when he had sinned. He thought that the men of Egypt would kill him and take his wife Sarai, so he told her to say that she was his sister, 12.11-13. Abram should not have gone to Egypt, and when he was there he should have trusted Jehovah to take care of him. Instead of that he thought he was wise enough to keep out of trouble by telling this lie. Pharaoh the king of Egypt believed that Sarai was Abram's sister and he took her for his wife. He gave Abram many animals and servants because of Sarai, 12.14-16. Then the Lord came in to help Abram. He made trouble for Pharaoh and Pharaoh understood that he had taken another man's wife. Pharaoh gave Abram back his wife and sent them back to Canaan in shame and disgrace, 12.17-20.

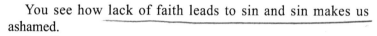 You see how lack of faith leads to sin and sin makes us ashamed.

1. Abram was afraid he might die of hunger so he went to Egypt.
2. There he was afraid he would be killed for his wife, so he lied about her.
3. The Lord saved him but a heathen man made Abram ashamed. It is a sad thing when the world must tell a believer that he has done what is wrong.

Abram and Lot, chapter 13

2/10 Abram went back to Bethel, 13.1-4, the place where he had built an altar to the Lord before, 12.8.

This teaches us an important lesson. If a believer falls into sin he must get back as quickly as possible to the place where the Lord can bless him, 1 John 1.9.

God had promised to give the land of Canaan to Abram but he lived there all his life as a stranger, Hebrews 11.9. Abram lived in tents, 12.8; 13.3; 18.1; and built altars, 12.7,8; 13.18; 22.9. He was a stranger in this world but a friend of God.

Lot was the son of Abram's brother. He travelled with Abram from Ur to Haran, to Canaan, to Egypt and back to Canaan. Lot knew that God had revealed Himself to Abram, but Lot did not learn to love God as Abram did.

Perhaps it was Lot or his wife who wanted Abram to go from Canaan to Egypt when everybody was hungry. Abram was put to shame in Egypt and learned his lesson, but Lot and his wife thought Egypt was a wonderful place.

When Abram and Lot returned from Egypt they were both very wealthy, 13.2,5, but this does not mean that they were happy. Money does not help us to grow spiritually. Abram and Lot both had a lot of cattle and there was a struggle between the men who looked after Abram's cattle and those who looked after Lot's.

In verse 7 the Holy Spirit added that the Canaanites were there and no doubt they saw this quarrel. When Christians fight ✳ or quarrel among themselves the world just looks on and laughs.

2/11 Abram did not want to quarrel with Lot. He suggested that they should divide their cattle and not try to live together. Abram was the older man and he could have chosen first, but he gave the first choice to Lot, 13.8,9.

Lot was quite willing to leave Abram and he decided to live in the plain of Jordan, 13.10,11, because there was plenty of water and grass for his cattle. Lot thought that the plain of Jordan looked like the Garden of Eden, and he remembered that Adam did not have to work hard while he was in Eden.

Lot also thought the plain of Jordan looked like the land of Egypt. In ✳ the Old Testament Egypt is a picture of this world and Lot was attracted to it. Lot did not think about the evil life of men in Sodom and Gomorrah nor their bad effect on himself, his wife and his children, 13.13. He chose the plain of Jordan so his cattle would have plenty to eat, but we soon see him living in cities and getting closer to Sodom itself, 13.12. Lot chose the plain of Jordan but he got Sodom as well.

Christian fathers should think of their children when they have to move to another place. Young lives are easily influenced for good or evil. Lot may have gained many more cattle when he moved to the plain of Jordan but he lost his children.

2/12 God spoke to Abram again after Lot had gone away. God told Abram to look over the whole land because He would give it to him and to his descendants for ever. Abram's descendants would be like the dust of the earth because no one would be able to count them. So Abram lived at Mamre for a while, 13.14-18.

Abram always got a blessing when he lived separately from the world and in fellowship with God. We have seen that he left the land of promise and went down to Egypt and fell into sin. Later we will see him going to Abimelech, king of Gerar, and again lying about his wife, 20.1-13. Here in chapter 13 we see him living in the land which God had promised. Every believer will get a blessing when he walks with God and stays separate

from the world.

Abram and Melchizedek, chapters 14, 15

2/13 Some believers want to share in the pleasures of this world, but then they must also expect to receive God's judgment when it comes on the world. This was the experience of Lot. In chapter 14 we read about four great kings from the east who came up against the land of Canaan and made the people pay taxes to them.

After twelve years the five kings of Canaan rebelled and refused to pay their taxes. The four kings came from the east to fight with them and they defeated the kings of Sodom, Gomorrah, and the other cities of Canaan. They took all the people as prisoners and also took their property. Lot and his family were among the prisoners.

2/14 Abram heard about this and he wanted to save his nephew, Lot. Abram had only 318 servants but some of his neighbors went with him. They attacked the four kings and all their men at night. God gave the victory to Abram and his friends. They delivered the prisoners, got back all their property and delivered Lot and his family, 14.13-16.

In verse 13 Abram is called the *Hebrew* which means he was a descendant of Eber who was still living, 11.16,17. The word Hebrew also means "one who has crossed over". Abram had left his home in Ur and was living separate from the people in the land of Canaan.

Any believer can walk with God, separated from the world. Those who do have the power of God can overcome their enemies. So here we see Lot a prisoner of the world and Abram a victor over the world.

2/15 Abram returned from the battle and two kings met him: Bera the king of Sodom and Melchizedek the king of Salem, 14.17,18. Salem was later called Jerusalem, and Melchizedek the king of Salem was also the priest of the Most High God. Melchizedek met Abram and gave him bread and wine. He blessed Abram in the name of the Most High God, and Abram gave him a tenth of all the property he had taken back from the four kings.

The name Melchizedek means *king of righteousness*. Salem means *peace*, so he was also *king of peace*. Notice that Melchizedek was both king and priest. Later we read in the Bible about many kings and many priests, but Melchizedek was the only person who was both king and priest. In this way he is a wonderful picture of our Lord Jesus Christ who is Priest and King as well as God's Prophet.

When Abram returned after this great struggle he was tired with the long hard journey. Melchizedek met him and gave him bread and wine and Abram felt stronger again. Melchizedek also blessed Abram in the name of Most High God. This made Abram stronger in his spirit.

Melchizedek helped Abram in a spiritual way and Abram gave Melchizedek a gift of money and other things which he had brought back. It is right that we should give gifts to those who help us understand the Word of God, 1 Corinthians 9.11.

The Lord Jesus Christ was a priest after the order of Melchizedek, Psalm 110.4; Hebrews 6.20; 7.17. God had commanded Moses that only men in the tribe of Levi should be priests of Israel. All the true kings of Israel belong to the tribe of Judah. Our Lord Jesus Christ was born in the tribe of Judah and He could not be a priest in the tribe of Levi. When He went back to heaven He became a priest for ever in the order of Melchizedek.

Then the king of Sodom met Abram and offered to give him all the *property* if Abram would give him all the *people* of his city, 14.21-24. Abram did not want to take anything belonging to this wicked man or his people. Here again Abram acted in faith and this is another victory for him. Melchizedek had blessed him in the name of God and this was more important to Abram than the things of this world. Abram had already learned that money does not always bring peace and joy.

Lot, however, had not learned this lesson. He could have stayed with Abram, the man of faith, but instead he decided to go back to Sodom again, 19.1.

2/16   Abram's victories were followed by another great promise from God, 15.1. God would be like a shield and would protect him when his enemies tried to strike him. Abram's reward would be very great because God Himself would be with him.

But then Abram began to ask the Lord about a son, 15.2,3. Eliezer was the chief slave in charge of Abram's property, and Abram did not want to think that a slave would one day have everything for himself. The Lord had already promised Abram that he would have a son and many descendants, 12.2,7; 13.15. In 13.16 He said that Abram's descendants would be like the dust of the earth. Now He promised that they would be like the stars of heaven. Abram believed this promise and God counted his faith as righteousness, 15.6.

In the New Testament many Jews tried to teach that people had to keep the law and be circumcised to be saved. The Holy Spirit led the apostle Paul to teach that we are saved by faith alone. Paul pointed out that Abram believed and God counted his faith for righteousness. This was long before the law was given and even before Abram was circumcised, Genesis 17.24. We too are counted righteous when we believe in the Lord Jesus Christ, Romans 4.1-5, 9,10; Galatians 3.6-9.

Abram believed God's promise but he asked for a sign, 15.8. God told him to take three animals: a young cow, a she-goat, a ram, and two birds. Abram killed these but did not burn them as sacrifices, 15.8-11. **2/17** The Lord told him he would one day own the land of Canaan, 15.7, but before that his children would be slaves in Egypt for about 400 years. Then the Lord would bring them into Canaan, 15.13,14; Exodus 12.40,41. Abram himself would live to old age, 15.15; 25.7,8.

God was going to punish the Amorites who lived in the land of Canaan because of their great sin. Then He would give the land to the children of Abram in the fourth generation, 15.16. God knew that the Amorites would be very wicked, but He would not destroy them until it was plain to everyone that their lives were evil.

God sent fire on Abram's sacrifice as a sign to strengthen his faith. Then He told him his descendants would have a large land from the river of Egypt on the south, to the river Euphrates on the north, 15.17,18. Nine nations besides the Amorites would be put out of this land because of their sin, 15.19-21.

God is never in a hurry. Some men go on sinning because they think that God will not judge them. Some believers lose heart because they think God has forgotten His promises. We have only to wait for God's time and then we will see His judgment on sin and His promises to us who believe. Let us be sure we have faith like Abram, for if we do we will be blessed with him also, Galatians 3.14.

Abram and Ishmael, chapters 16, 17

Patience / God's timing

2/18 Abram believed that God would give him a son but he did not wait for God's time. Sarai his wife suggested that he should take Hagar, her Egyptian servant as his wife. She said perhaps Hagar would become the mother of the promised son. Abram listened to Sarai and took Hagar as his second wife. Soon Hagar knew that she would have a child. She became proud and looked down on Sarai. Sarai and Abram had both done wrong but Sarai blamed Abram for her trouble, 16.5. Abram told her that she could do as she pleased to Hagar, and the result was that Hagar ran away, 16.6.

Sin.

Sin

It is God's will that a man should have only one wife, Genesis 2.24; Titus 1.6. In the Old Testament we read of many men of faith who took more than one wife but they always had trouble in the home.

2/19 God saw that Abram's faith had failed again, but still He looked after Hagar because she would be the mother of Abram's first son. The angel of the Lord told Hagar to go back to Sarai. The Lord knew that Sarai had not been fair to Hagar, and anyway this boy would really be a son of Abram. Hagar should call her son Ishmael. He would have many children, but he would be a wild man, an enemy of everybody else, 16.9-12. Hagar believed that God saw her and had spoken to her and she went back to Sarai.

Abram was 86 years old when the baby was born, 16.15,16. Abram too believed that God had spoken to Hagar and he called the boy's name Ishmael. Ishmael was not the child that God had promised to Abraham; he was the child of the flesh and an enemy of the child of promise, Galatians 4.23,29. Today it is the same; people of this world are enemies of the true children of faith. We are dead to the world and the world is dead to us, Galatians 6.14.

2/20 Abram had to wait many more years before his true son would be born. When he was 99 years old God came to him again and revealed Himself as the *Almighty* God, 17.1.

God had already revealed Himself to Abram through Melchizedek as the *Most High God*, 14.18-20. Later Abraham learned that Jehovah was the *everlasting God*, 21.33. After that he learned that Jehovah will provide, 22.14. Whenever Abraham believed in God and took a step of faith he learned more about what God is like. We can have the same experience.

God told Abram to live with Him and be perfect and He would make a covenant with him, 17.2-8. Abram fell down to worship and God continued to speak to him. Abram would be the ancestor of many nations, not of only one. God changed his name to Abraham which means *the father of many people*. Some of his descendants would be kings and God's covenant with them would never come to an end. Abraham's descendants would possess the land of Canaan for ever and Jehovah would be their God, 17.8. In the rest of the Bible the name Abraham is almost always used.

2/21 God has made many covenants with men at different times. Some covenants are agreements that God will do certain things *if* man does his part. This kind of an agreement is called a *conditional* covenant. Sometimes God makes a covenant in which *He* promises to do something for man. This is an *unconditional* covenant because there are no conditions for man to fulfill.

In this case God does not tell us what to do but simply promises what *He* is going to do. His covenant with Abraham, 17.2,7, was unconditional. All that Abraham and his descendants have to do is to believe God's promise. Even if they don't believe, God is still going to fulfill His word.

God told Abraham to circumcise every man and boy in his family including his servants, as a sign of God's covenant. This would show that they belonged to the family of Abraham and were under the covenant of God. Anyone who was not circumcised had to be put out, 17.9-14.

2/22 The sign of circumcision became so important to the Jews that many tried to force it on the early Christians as well. The apostle Paul went out preaching the gospel, and Jews followed him everywhere telling the new Christians that they had to be circumcised to be saved. The apostle Paul taught that they were saved by grace alone, Galatians 5.3,4; Ephesians 2.8,9.

Then God changed Sarai's name to Sarah and promised once more that she would have a son. Abraham was sure that he and Sarah were too old to have children and he just laughed at God's promise, 17.17. He prayed that God would give the special blessing to Ishmael, 17.18. Once again God had to tell him that Sarah herself would have a son and his name would be Isaac. God's covenant would be with Isaac and his descendants. However, He said he would answer Abraham's prayer about Ishmael, and his descendants would become a great nation also. Isaac was born about a year later, 17.21.

Abraham's prayer in verse 18 shows that he did not really believe God and the results of that prayer were terrible. The descendants of Ishmael turned out to be great enemies of the people of Israel. Even today some people think that the Arabs are the descendants of Ishmael, and certainly they are bitter enemies of the Jews. We should be very careful to pray according to the will of God and in the name of the Lord Jesus.

Abraham took Ishmael and all the men of his house and circumcised them. Abraham was 99 years old at this time and Ishmael was 13. Circumcision became a law for the descendants of Abraham, but it is not a law for Christians today. We are saved by grace alone without works.

You must not add anything to the finished work of Christ on the cross. You must not add circumcision, law-keeping, Sabbath-keeping, baptism or any other works. The Bible says that we are not saved by righteous works, Titus 3.5. Every Christian should be baptized, but baptism is only a sign to others that you have been saved.

Now test yourself

[handwritten margin note: No: Should have gone straight to Canaan but delayed in Haman]

1. Abraham traveled to Haran, to Canaan, and to Egypt. In which of these journeys did Abraham fully obey God? *[handwritten: Canaan — God told him to go there]*

[handwritten margin note: No: Took his family too & God said leave family behind]

2. Why did Lot choose to live in the plain of Jordan? *[handwritten: Looked good for cattle, like garden of Eden.]*

3. How is Melchizedek a picture of our Lord Jesus Christ? *[handwritten: Priest + King — Priest of God most high, & King of peace + rightea]*

4. Abraham believed God's promise and his faith was counted for righteousness. Which promise was that? *[handwritten: Descendants too many to count, like stars in heavens.]*

[handwritten margin note: No: Told Sara to act as sister]

5. Why did Abraham take Hagar to be his wife? *[handwritten: Wanted the son God had promised. Sarai gave Hagar to him + he was impatient so accepted]*

6. What is an unconditional covenant? *[handwritten: Man does not need to fulfil anything for God to keep his promise.]*

Turn to page 114 to check your answers.

- 5 -

MORE ABOUT ABRAHAM
chapters 18 - 21

2/23 *We have seen that God taught Abram many lessons and changed his name to Abraham. In this lesson we will learn more about Abraham and Lot, Abimelech, Isaac and Ishmael.*

The friend of God, chapter 18

Abraham is the only man in the Bible who is called a "friend of God", 2 Chronicles 20.7; Isaiah 41.8; James 2.23. We have seen that Abraham obeyed God's call and believed God's promises. God loves people who believe His word, and obey His commands.

In chapter 18 we read about Abraham talking to the Lord as friend to friend. Three men came to Abraham's tent about the middle of the day. Abraham did not know who they were, but he welcomed them as visitors. He asked them to rest a little while until he got some food ready for them to eat. The visitors agreed to this and Sarah and the servant helped Abraham get things ready, 18.1-8. One of these three was Jehovah Himself. This is the third time that Jehovah appeared to Abraham, 12.7; 17.1.

2/24 In verses 9-15 Jehovah again promised Abraham that Sarah his wife would have a son. Both Abraham and Sarah were already old and when Sarah heard these words she laughed in her heart, just as Abraham had done before, 17.17. She did not think that these men would hear her, but of course the Lord knows the heart. He asked why Sarah laughed and told her that nothing is too hard for the Lord, 18.14. Sarah denied that she had laughed, but it was true.

It is a terrible thing to laugh at God or to refuse to believe His promises. God created the heavens and the earth and nothing is too hard for Him, Luke 1.37.

2/25 The Lord Jesus calls His disciples *friends* because He told them all things, John 15.15. Here in verses 16-21 Jehovah revealed to Abraham His friend what He was going to do to Sodom. But first He told Abraham again that He would make his descendants into a great nation. He knew that Abraham would command his children to follow the Lord.

The Lord knew that the sin of the men of Sodom and Gomorrah was very great and these cities must be destroyed. But first He came down in His mercy to see for Himself, 18.20,21. The two other persons with Jehovah were really angels in the form of men. They went off to Sodom, 18.22, to give the people of the city one last chance. However the wickedness of the hearts of the men of Sodom was fully revealed.

2/26 Abraham did not want Lot and his family to die with the people of Sodom. He asked the Lord if He would destroy righteous men as well as those who were wicked, 18.23-33. Abraham perhaps thought that Lot had told the men of Sodom about the Lord and at least a few had turned to God. He asked the Lord to spare the city if there were fifty righteous people in it. Jehovah said that He would spare the whole city if there were fifty righteous people in Sodom.

Then Abraham began to wonder if Lot had been able to win this number of people for the Lord. He asked Jehovah if He would spare the city for forty-five people. God granted this also. Then Abraham cut it down to forty, then thirty, then twenty, and then ten. Jehovah agreed to all this and promised to spare the whole city if there were ten righteous people in it. Abraham might have thought that Lot's wife, his daughters and his sons and sons-in-law would at least make up the total of ten. As it turned out there were not ten righteous persons in Sodom. Still Jehovah did what Abraham really desired in his heart: He saved Lot as well as his wife and his two unmarried daughters.

In this chapter we see Abraham, the friend of God, receiving Jehovah and two angels in his home. God revealed to Abraham as a friend what He was going to do. Abraham felt free to speak with the Lord and pray to Him about Lot.

In the New Testament we are told to go into the most holy place and come near to God, Hebrews 10.19-22. We should pray for God's people; this is what the Lord Jesus is doing. He lives to pray for us, Hebrews 7.25, so we are very like Him when we pray for the people of the Lord. Sometimes we do not know how to pray as we should, Romans 8.26, but we can be sure that the Judge of all the earth will do what is right, Genesis 18.25.

This last verse gives us peace as we face many problems in the world today. Wicked people seem to get along very well and righteous people often have to suffer. There is also a problem about those who have never heard the gospel. Will God judge them the same as others who have heard and rejected Christ? In all these things we can be sure that *God the Judge of all the earth will do right.* ✳

God destroyed Sodom and Gomorrah, chapter 19

2/27 Sin in the world is like an evil growth in the human body. A doctor must cut it out or it will quickly spread through the body and the person will die. The cities of Sodom and Gomorrah were so wicked that God decided to destroy them. This was the only way to keep the evil from spreading through the land.

In 19.1-11 we see that the two angels came to Sodom in the evening and found Lot sitting with the judges in the gateway of the city. At first Lot had gone to the valley of Jordan so he could feed his cattle but soon he was drawn to the wicked cities. Then we read that he had a place of honor among those sinful men.

Lot showed kindness to the visitors, as Abraham had done. At first the visitors refused to stay with him, but he urged them and they agreed to stay. But before they lay down for the night, the wicked men of the city came and demanded that Lot should give the visitors to them for their evil purposes. Lot called them "brothers" and asked them to change their minds. He offered to give them his two daughters for their wicked desires. Lot had kept these daughters from the evil men of the city until then, but now he wanted to save his visitors and was willing to give his daughters to the men of Sodom. He knew that these visitors were not ordinary men.

Lot had known that the men of Sodom were very wicked and that he should not live with them. Perhaps he had tried to make things better but, if so, he certainly had not succeeded. The people of Sodom laughed at him and said he came as a visitor, and now he wanted to be judge and to tell them what to do, 19.9. They would have attacked Lot but the angels inside made them blind and pulled Lot into the house.

It is equally useless for Christians today to try to make the world better. Our duty is to bring men to Christ. He alone can change hearts. ✳

Some people used to think that the sin of Sodom was the worst sin. Others argued that adultery or murder was the worst. We should remember that other sins like pride and false teaching are very serious. We know from the Bible that *all* sin is rebelling against the will of God and only Christ can forgive and deliver us from the power of sin.

2/28 This event proves beyond all doubt that the men of Sodom were very wicked. The angels prepared to carry out the command of the Lord by destroying the city, 19.12-14. They gave Lot a little time until morning to warn his family. But Lot's sons-in-law just laughed at him.

Some Christians try to live like the people of the world but they can never win anyone for the Lord. They only make themselves look foolish. This does not mean that we have to live by ourselves on an island. We should be friendly with people, but we cannot go along with their worldly practices and sinful habits.

In the morning the angels told Lot to hurry, 19.15-23. Still Lot waited, until at last they took him, his wife, and daughters by the hand and brought them out of the city. Then they told Lot to hurry to the mountains so he would not be destroyed with Sodom. Lot was afraid to go to the mountains so he asked them to spare the city of Zoar. Lot said that Zoar was just a little city, 19.20, but it was one of the five main cities around Sodom, 14.2. The angels granted this request and spared the city. So the evil was not completely rooted out and in later years it spread again through all Canaan. God had to command His people Israel to destroy these nations because of their evil, Deuteronomy 18.9,12.

2/29 At last Lot entered Zoar and the fire came down from Jehovah out of heaven and destroyed the other cities and all the people of the plain, 19.24-28. Lot's wife was saved from the fire but she looked back to Sodom with sorrow. Her heart was still in the wicked city and she too was destroyed, 19.26.

Lot's wife was not a believer. A true believer can never be lost again, but he will suffer the Father's chastening if he turns back. This should be a warning to those who have been saved; we should never look back to the world, Luke 17.32. Later God delivered the Israelites from Egypt but they looked back on the pleasures they had enjoyed there, Numbers 11.5. This did not please the Lord.

Abraham was in the hills above the plain and he saw with his own eyes how God destroyed these wicked men, but he himself was spared, 19.27,28. See Psalm 91.7,8.

2/30 Lot's troubles were not over. His daughters had learned very well the lessons of the world in Sodom, 19.31-35. First they made their father drunk with wine so that he could not think clearly for himself, then the daughters went in to lie with him. The result was that Lot was the father of his daughters' sons, Moab and Ben-Ammi. The descendants of Lot were called the Moabites and the Ammonites. They were the enemies of the people of Israel all through their history.

Christians should bring up their children for the Lord and not in the pleasures of this world. Those who bring them up in the pleasures of this world may live to be very sorry about it.

This is the sad end of the story of Lot. In the New Testament we read that he was a good man, 2 Peter 2.7,8. He knew the promises of God and in part he believed in them. He chose to live with the world and so he suffered with the world. He was troubled in his heart when he saw the terrible behavior of the wicked men of Sodom. He could have left Sodom at any time if he had really tried. Perhaps his wife would not leave. Lot refused all God's warnings and his life ended in deep shame.

Abraham and Abimelech, chapter 20

3/1 A believer may not always gain victory over evil. We may get our eyes off the Lord and then we are certain to fall into sin. We should be especially careful after a time of victory because it is just then that Satan will try to make us fall. The Bible tells us that the greatest saints fell into sin at times, and the only perfect Man who ever lived was the Lord Jesus Christ.

Abraham the friend of God saw from a high place the judgment of the world. He then moved on toward the south and came to a country of the Philistines. Once again he was afraid that men would kill him because of his wife, 12.12. Again he lied as he had done in Egypt, and said that Sarah was his sister. So Abimelech took her to be his wife, 20.1,2.

God in His mercy warned Abimelech and told him to give Sarah back to Abraham. God knew that both Abraham and Sarah had lied but He told Abimelech to give Sarah back to her husband. If Abimelech did not do this he and his family would all die, 20.3-7.

3/2 Abimelech called Abraham and told him he had done wrong, 20.8-18. Abraham tried to explain by saying that Sarah was **3/3** his *half* sister, 20.12. Abimelech gave Abraham many gifts and told him he could live anywhere in his land, 20.14-16. Then Abraham prayed for Abimelech and the Lord healed the women of Abimelech's family.

We see that Abraham and Sarah agreed together to tell this lie, 20.5,13. What they said was partly true but a half truth is a half lie. They just could not trust God to look after them. We can also see in verse 13 that Abraham was not trusting the Lord because he said God *caused* him to wander from his father's house. It was really the grace of God that brought Abraham from Ur to Canaan.

Abraham thought that Abimelech and his family did not fear God, 20.11, but they really showed more faith than Abraham himself. Still Abraham was a prophet of God and he could pray for the Gentile king. God had promised to bless those who bless Abraham, 12.3, and God always does what He has promised.

We can see again in this chapter how Satan tried to break up Abraham's home. God had promised that Abraham and Sarah would have a son and all the nations of the world would be blessed in him. Satan is always seeking to spoil God's plan if he can.

Isaac was born, chapter 21

3/4   The name Isaac means *laughter* and it shows how happy his father was when God carried out His promise after so many years. Abraham was 100 years old, and he lived another 75 years, 25.7. Sarah also was very happy when the baby was born. She was over 90 at this time and she lived to be 127, 17.17; 23.1.

3/5   Abraham made a great feast when Isaac was a little older. Of course Hagar and Ishmael were not happy about Isaac. They knew that *he* would be the heir of Abraham according to God's promise. Sarah saw Ishmael and Isaac together and she knew that there would be trouble; in fact, Ishmael persecuted Isaac, Galatians 4.29. Sarah asked Abraham to send Hagar and Ishmael away. Abraham did not want this but God told him to do so. *Isaac* was the child of promise, but God said He would also make Ishmael into a great nation. So Abraham obeyed the word of the Lord and sent Hagar and Ishmael away, 21.8-14.

Hagar and Sarah are pictures of law and grace, Galatians 4.21-31. Many people still teach that we must keep the law if we wish to be saved. They do not believe that God will save us by grace alone, and there's always a struggle between law and grace. A true believer must put away all thoughts of winning God's favor by keeping the law. This is the only way to have peace.

3/6   Hagar wandered around in the desert until all her water was gone, and she thought Ishmael would die. The angel of God heard Ishmael and told Hagar that God would make him into a great nation.

The angel showed her where she could get water and so Ishmael did not die of thirst at that time, 21.15-21.

Abimelech king of Gerar had learned that God was with Abraham, 20.7; 21.22, and he wanted Abraham to be fair with him and with his children. Abraham was willing to promise this, but he told Abimelech that his servants had taken Abraham's well, 21.23-25. Abimelech gave the well back to Abraham, 21.26-30, and they both promised to keep the peace. They called that place Beersheba which means the *well of the oath*. Abraham planted a tree there and called on the name of Jehovah, the everlasting God.

3/7 Abraham had learned before that Jehovah was the *Most High* God, 14.18,19. This name tells us that God is supreme over heaven and earth. Then God revealed Himself as the *Almighty God* or El-Shaddai, 17.1. This name teaches us the power of God and also His loving care for His children. Just as a mother feeds her baby so God looks after those who trust in Him. In this chapter Abraham learned that Jehovah is the *everlasting* God. This means that God always was and always will be. No one created God and no one can destroy Him. From eternity past to eternity future God is God, Psalm 90.2.

God is the greatest Person in heaven and earth and our greatest blessing is to know Him. In the Old Testament we read many different names of God, but we learn more about His love and wisdom in the New Testament. *And this is eternal life, to know You, the only true God, and Jesus Christ, whom You sent,* John 17.3.

Now test yourself

1. Who is called a friend of God?

   — abraham ✓

   Who are called friends by the Lord Jesus?

   — His disciples. ✓

2. Did Jehovah answer Abraham's prayer about the city of Sodom? *Yes, he wanted God to save Lot this family and God did this.* ✓

3. Lot was a righteous man, 2 Peter 2.7,8. Did he have a good influence in wicked Sodom? *No, no-one followed God by* ✓ *copying him & even Lots son-in laws wouldn't believe*

4. Name two children who were Lot's sons and also his grand- *him.* sons. *Moab & Ben-Ammi* ✓.

5. What sin did Abraham fall into twice? *Twice he called Sarah his sister instead of wife.* ✓

6. What are the three names of God which Abraham learned?

Turn to page 114 to check your answers.

① *Most High God.* ✓

② *El Shaddai / God Almighty.* ✓

③ *Everlasting God.* ✓

- 6 -

MORE ABOUT ABRAHAM
chapters 22 - 24

3/8 *Abraham by now had learned many lessons in his life with God; we may say, in the school of God. We notice that Jehovah appeared to him three times, and spoke to him five other times. In every case God spoke about Abraham's son or his descendants, and said they would be like the dust of the earth, the stars of heaven, and the grains of sand on the edge of the sea. Abraham believed the promise of God and it was counted to him for righteousness, 15.6. He is called the friend of God and the father of all who believe, Romans 4.11.*

GENESIS, chapter	12	13	15	17	18	21	22
God and Abraham							
God appeared to Abraham, v.	7			1	1		
God spoke to Abraham, v.	1	14	1			12	1
About his descendants, v.	2,7	15	5	7	10	12	17
He said they would be like		dust, 16	stars, 5				sand, 17

Abraham's sacrifice, chapter 22

Still we have seen that Abraham's faith failed many times. He went down to Egypt, 12.10; he said that Sarah was his sister, 12.19; 20.2; he questioned God's promises, 15.2; 17.18; and he could not wait for God's time, 16.4.

Abraham had failed but he had learned well many of his lessons. By now God, the Great Teacher, saw that His child Abraham was ready for a hard test, 22.1. We must not think that God *tried* to make Abraham sin, James 1.13. Satan tries to make us sin and he is called the tempter, but God did put Abraham to the test.

God still tests His children and sometimes the greatest Christians suffer terribly. In Genesis 22 Abraham brought glory to God and we can do the same if we obey His commands without question.

One night God told Abraham to take his son, his only son, his beloved son, and offer him for a burnt offering. This was the child God had promised and for whom Abraham had waited so many years. When he was born his father and mother were so happy that they called him Isaac: "laughter."

Why did God command His faithful servant to offer up his son? God later told Moses and His people Israel not to follow the wicked custom of the nations around them who sacrificed their children in fire, Deuteronomy 12.31. Yet here God commanded Abraham to do this. Why?

Perhaps God wanted one father, Abraham, to understand His own feelings when He offered His only Son as a sacrifice for sins. Mount Moriah is where the temple was later built in Jerusalem, 2 Chronicles 3.1. The Lord Jesus Christ was crucified many years later near this very spot. God loves His Son. No man can understand how God felt when He offered His Son to suffer on the cross as a sacrifice for our sins. God will not ask any man to kill his son but we can understand in part how Abraham felt on Mount Moriah.

Abraham had learned by now that he should obey God's commands at once. He knew that God loved him and would give him nothing that was bad. So Abraham rose early in the morning, took Isaac his son, took two servants, some wood, some fire in a pot and a knife. They set out at once for the land of Moriah.

At first God told Abraham to go to the land of Moriah and then He would show him one of the mountains there, 22.2. God often tells us only part of the way at a time. When we obey He shows us more exactly where He wants us to go. We cannot know all the way from the beginning, but we should learn to obey quickly even when the future is dark.

Melchizedek was the king of Salem, the city later called Jerusalem. As Abraham started out for Moriah no doubt he remembered the spiritual blessing he had received from Melchizedek, 14.19. This would give him more strength for the trial which lay ahead. On the third day Abraham saw the place still far away. He left the two servants at that time and said, "Isaac and I will worship and we will come again to you," 22.4,5. Abraham showed that he had faith in God when he said we will come again. He knew that God would raise up Isaac from the dead, Hebrews 11.19.

True worship is possible for those who believe God's word and understand that He has given His Son for their sins.

The servants were not allowed to go all the way to the top of the mountain. Abraham was going to offer his son and he did not want anyone else to be there. So we, as men, will never know all that was in the heart of the Father and the Son at Calvary.

Carrying the wood was the work of the servants, and now Abraham asked his son Isaac to carry it. Isaac is a picture of God's Son who became the Servant, Matthew 12.18; Philippians 2.7. The father and the son went on together, 22.6. Isaac loved and trusted his father but he began to wonder about a lamb for a sacrifice. He knew the story of Cain and remembered that God had refused Cain's sacrifice because he did not bring an animal. Isaac asked Abraham about an animal for the offering. Abraham said that God would provide, 22.7,8,13. Later God did provide the Lamb of God to take away the sin of the world, John 1.29.

3/9 At last they came to the place and gathered stones together for an altar. Abraham laid the wood in order on the altar and Isaac must have known by then what was going to take place. He did not struggle or try to run away. He was like the Son of God, he obeyed his father's command. *I always do what pleases Him,* John 8.29

Think of Isaac's feelings as he saw the wood, the knife and the fire, as his father tied him and laid him on the altar! Think how Abraham felt as he took the knife in his hand ready to kill his own son, the one whom God had promised! Here we have a faint picture of how God and Christ felt. Let us worship the Lord as we think of how Christ suffered at the hand of God. God said He would strike the Shepherd, Matthew 26.31, and the Lord Jesus took His sufferings as from His Father, *The cup which my Father has given me,* John 18.11.

But just at that minute the Angel of the Lord called Abraham. Abraham had shown clearly that he would obey God in everything, so the Angel told him that the test was over, 22.12, 13. Abraham saw a male sheep caught in a low tree and he offered up the sheep instead of his son.

No man or animal could die instead of the Lord Jesus when God offered *His* Son. Christ had to die for us.

Abraham knew by faith that God would provide an animal, 22.8. He had seen God supply a ram to die instead of his son so he gave the place a new name, 22.14.

3/10   Abraham came through this test so well that God gave him still another promise. The Angel said that Abraham's descendants would be like the stars of heaven and like the sand at the edge of the sea in number. Abraham had many natural descendants, but the promise really refers to believers of all ages, Romans 4.16; Galatians 3.7. His descendants would gain the victory over their enemies, 22.17, but God would bless all nations through Abraham's Son, the Lord Jesus Christ. Read Acts 3.25 and Galatians 3.16, and you will see that verse 18 really means Christ. The Lord Jesus gave Himself for the sins of all nations, 1 John 2.2.

Who is this Angel of the Lord, 22.11,15? The word "angel" means "messenger," but the Angel of the Lord is the Son of God, speaking for God. The Angel of the Lord used the word "I" when speaking as God in 16.10; 21.18; and 22.12. The Son of God can say with truth, "I and the Father are one," John 10.30. Isaac is a picture of the Lord Jesus Christ when He died, and the Son of God was very much interested in these events.

In this chapter we learn something of how God felt when He gave His Son and how Christ felt when He suffered at the hands of God. We also learn from both Abraham and Isaac that God blesses those who obey Him.

Then Abraham returned to Beersheba and lived there. The rest of this chapter tells us about the family of Nahor, Abraham's brother who had not come to Palestine with him, 11.27-31. The most important name in verses 20 to 24 is Rebekah, the daughter of Bethuel, the son of Milcah. We shall read more about Rebekah in chapter 24.

The death of Sarah, chapter 23

3/11   Here we read that Sarah died when she had reached the age of 127 years. Abraham bought a field from one of the Hittites for Sarah's grave, 23.4-16. These verses show that Abraham was very kind and polite when he did business with the men around him, but he would not take anything from them without paying for it. The Lord God had given him the whole land but he was still a stranger in it, Hebrews 11.9. God's time had not yet come when Abraham would possess the land for himself.

3/12   We are strangers in this world, 1 Peter 2.11. We should obey the laws of the government, and pay all taxes, Romans 13.1, 6. Still we should be separate from the world and not take part in its evil practices.

The land really belonged to Abraham but he was willing to pay a price for it. This is a little picture of how God saves us. We men belong to God because He created us, yet Christ was willing to pay the price that we might be redeemed, or bought back, for God.

A bride for the son, chapter 24

3/13 After Abraham had buried Sarah he began to think about a wife for his son who by then was nearly forty years old. Abraham called his oldest servant and made him promise to get a wife for Isaac. Abraham did not want his son to marry a Canaanite girl because the people of the land did not believe in Jehovah. The servant should go back to Abraham's country and God would help him get a wife for Isaac. In chapter 24 we do not read the name of this servant but it may have been Eliezer, 15.2. He promised with an oath to do what Abraham desired, but if no girl was willing to come back with him he would be free from his oath, 24.1-9.

Later on God gave His law to Moses and commanded the people of Israel not to marry a near relative. At this time Abraham was not breaking God's law by getting a wife for Isaac from his own family. Still later the Lord Jesus commanded us not to swear nor take an oath, Matthew 5.34-37. We should not swear we will do something at a future time because everything is in God's power, James 4.13-15.

3/14 The servant had charge of all Abraham's property. He took a few servants, ten camels for them to ride on, and some beautiful gifts for Isaac's bride. After a long journey they arrived at the city of Nahor. The servant wanted to be sure of the Lord's will so he asked for a sign, 24.10-14. He prayed that the girl whom the Lord had chosen would offer to draw water for all his camels. Ten camels, after a long journey across the desert, need a great deal of water. Most girls would have been willing to draw water for the travelers but would have expected the servants to draw water for all the camels.

3/15 He was still praying when at that very minute, beautiful Rebekah came to draw water, 24.15-21. She gave water to Abraham's servant and *offered* to draw more water for the camels. The servant watched in silence but he was very happy that the Lord had answered his prayer in such a wonderful way.

3/16 Then the servant gave Rebekah three very valuable ornaments of gold. He asked her what was the name of her father and if they could stay that night at her father's house. She told him that she was the daughter of Bethuel, the son of Nahor. Then the servant knew that the Lord had heard his prayer. He could not answer Rebekah so she continued and told him that there was room and food enough for all. The servant gave thanks to Jehovah for leading him in the right way, 24.22-27.

It is still the same today. God will guide those who are willing to follow and they will know what is right, John 7.17.

Rebekah ran back to the house. Laban her brother saw the ornaments of gold and heard her story. He went out and asked Abraham's servant to stay with them, 24.28-33. The servant entered their home but he would not eat any food until he had explained his message.

3/17 The man told Laban that he was Abraham's servant, that the Lord had blessed Abraham with great wealth, and that he had given everything to Isaac. Then he told how he had come across the desert to get a bride for Isaac and how the Lord had led him to Rebekah, 24.34-49. Rebekah's brother and father agreed that the Lord had been guiding him and they were willing to let Rebekah go with the servant, 24.50,51.

3/18 The servant brought out more gold and silver and clothing for Rebekah. He also gave gifts to her brother and her mother, 24.52,53. The servant wanted to start back on the long journey the very next day because he knew that Isaac would be waiting for them. Rebekah's family wanted her to stay for a while but she agreed to go with the man and become Isaac's wife. Rebekah's brother and father blessed her and Rebekah and her maidens were soon ready to go, 24.54-61.

Abraham's servant was a man of faith. He asked Jehovah to guide him and God answered in a wonderful way. The servant also wanted to do his master's will as quickly as possible. He would not even eat his food until he had stated his business, 24.33. Then he wanted to get back to Abraham and Isaac as soon as he could, 24.54,56. We should learn these lessons; the Lord Jesus loves a faithful servant, Matthew 25.21.

3/19 Finally the servant and the bride drew near. Isaac had gone out to the field in the evening. No doubt he was praying that they would get home safely. He looked up and saw the camels coming. Rebekah humbly covered herself with a veil. Isaac took her as his wife and loved her, 24.62-67.

All this is a beautiful picture of God, Christ and the Church. In chapter 22 we saw Abraham offering up his son as a sacrifice just as God did later on. Here the father sent the servant into a far country to get a bride for his son; it was the father's plan. The servant is not named and here he is a picture of the Holy Spirit. The servant had charge over all the father's riches, 24.10; and the Holy Spirit is equal with God. The Father sent the Spirit into this world and His work is to speak well of the Son, 24.36; John 16.14. The Son of God is the Heir of all things, Matthew 11.27; Hebrews 1.2.

These two chapters, 22 and 24, go together. The first time the word *love* is found in the Bible is 22.2, and the second time is 24.67. In the one verse we see the love of the Father for His Son, and in the other the love of Christ for His Church. Christ loved the Church, gave Himself for it, and He is now preparing the Church to present it to Himself as a perfect Bride, Ephesians 5.25-27. Also, the servant gave gifts to Rebekah and the Holy Spirit gives gifts to the Church according to His own will, 1 Corinthians 12.8-11.

The Father will not send the Son back into this world to get His Bride, 24.6, but Christ is waiting for us and is praying for His beloved, Hebrews 7.25. At the right time He will come to the clouds and meet us in the air, 1 Thessalonians 4.16,17. The servant told Isaac all things that he had done, 24.66, and we will give a report to the Lord at the Judgment Seat of Christ, Luke 19.15; Romans 14.10; 2 Corinthians 5.10. This will be followed by the wedding feast, Revelation 19.9. *So we will always be with the Lord. So then comfort one another with these words,* 1 Thessalonians 4.17,18.

Now test yourself

To test his faith. Also picture of God offering His own son as sacrifice.

1. Why did God tell Abraham to offer up his son Isaac as a sacrifice?

2. How did Abraham know that Isaac would come down from Mount Moriah with him? *Believed that God would raise him from dead.*

3. Who was the Angel of the Lord? 22.11,15. *God's son.*

4. God had given the whole land of Canaan to Abraham. Why then did he have to buy some ground before he could bury his wife when she died? *Still a stranger in the land. Not time for him to possess it yet so should still pay to current owners.*

5. Why did the servant of Abraham pray to God? *Wanted God to lead him to the correct girl for Isaac*

6. "In chapter 24 we have a picture of God, the Three-in-One." Explain this statement.

Turn to page 115 to check your answers.

Abraham = God / Father.
Servant = Holy Spirit
Isaac = Son of God (Jesus)

(Rebecca = bride / church / us).

- 7 -
ISAAC
chapters 25-27

3/20 *In the next three chapters Isaac is the most important person, but first we read about the end of Abraham's life.*

Later life and death of Abraham, 25.1-11

After Sarah died Abraham took another wife called Keturah, and she had many sons, 25.1-4. Abraham also took other women as his wives, but like Hagar they were not given the same honor as a true wife. Abraham did not seem to understand that God does not want a man to have more than one wife. Abraham had many sons and he gave them gifts, but he gave all his wealth to Isaac and sent the other sons away, 25.6. These sons had many descendants and some turned out to be the enemies of the people of Israel.

3/21 Abraham lived to be 175 years old. This would be a very great age today, but in the days of Genesis men lived to still greater ages. Before the Flood some men lived 800 or 900 years, but after the Flood men did not live so long. However, Eber, one of the ancestors of Abraham, lived to be 464 years old, 11.16,17. Eber lived three years after Abraham had died, and Abraham was called a Hebrew, which means the descendant of Eber, 14.13.

When Abraham died, Isaac and Ishmael buried him in the same place where Abraham had buried his wife Sarah, 25.9,10. God fulfilled His promise to Abraham and blessed his son Isaac, 25.11.

The sons of Ishmael, 25.12-18

3/22 Ishmael and Isaac were both sons of Abraham, but Isaac was the son who was born according to God's promise. We know nothing about Ishmael except what we learn in these seven verses. Ishmael had twelve sons, all princes, and he lived 137 years. Abraham had sent his sons toward the east country, 25.6, but Ishmael's sons went to live in the south, 25.18.

The sons of Isaac, 25.19-34

3/23 We read much more about Isaac in Genesis than we do about Ishmael. Isaac was forty years old when he married Rebekah but for twenty years they had no children. Then Isaac prayed for his wife and the Lord heard him.

Before the children were born they struggled together and Rebekah prayed to the Lord about this. The Lord told her that she would have not one son but two, and each of them would become a great nation. The struggle of the two babies would continue when they became men, but the younger one would be the greater. God knows all the future, and He told Rebekah that the older son would serve the younger one, 25.21-23.

The first baby boy was born covered with red hair and they called his name Esau. As the second was born his hand took hold of Esau's heel, so they called him Jacob, 25.24-26.

God had blessed Isaac with the blessing of Abraham, so Isaac knew that God would give him a son and would pass this blessing on to him. The Lord tested Isaac's faith and did not give him a son for twenty years. We must not think that those who believe in Christ will not have any trials. Both Isaac and Rebekah did right when they prayed to God. They did not understand what was happening but God answered them both.

3/24 The boys grew up and Esau became a clever hunter, but Jacob lived at home with his father and mother. Isaac loved Esau because he brought him wild meat to eat, but Rebekah loved Jacob, 25.27,28.

One day something happened which showed how both Esau and Jacob really felt, 25.29-34. Esau came home after hunting and was very tired and hungry. He saw Jacob cooking food and asked him to give him something to eat. Esau agreed to sell his *birthright* for a little food.

This birthright was a special privilege which belonged to the oldest son in the family. The oldest son would usually get two parts of the father's property, while the other sons got only one each, Deuteronomy 21.17, but the father could give the birthright to a younger son if the oldest son was not worthy. For example, Isaac received the promises which God had given to Abraham, although Ishmael was older than Isaac.

Abraham and his sons knew the most important thing was a spiritual blessing based on God's promise. This was of far greater value than all the cattle and sheep and silver and gold.

Esau was the older brother and should have had the blessing of the birthright, but God had promised that the younger son, Jacob, would be the greater. From this promise Jacob should have known that the birthright would be his, but he did not quite believe God's promise. Esau was a worldly man and had no interest in spiritual things, Hebrews 12.16. He thought he might die of hunger and then the birthright would be of no value to him anyway.

Jacob had a real desire for the spiritual blessing, but tried to get it by his own clever plan. Esau cared only for himself and the things of this world. Do you have a desire for spiritual blessing? You must be ready to wait for it. The Lord will send the blessing in His own time and in His own way.

Isaac and Abimelech, chapter 26

3/25 After this there was another famine in the land and people became very hungry. Isaac had to care for his family and also his many servants. In the earlier famine Abraham had gone down to Egypt, 12.10, but this time Isaac went to Abimelech, a friend of Abraham's 21.22-24. The Lord appeared to Isaac and told him not to go to Egypt but to stay in the land of Palestine, 26.1-5. Then the Lord told Isaac that He would bless him with the blessings of Abraham:

1. God would give the land of Palestine to Isaac and his sons.

2. Isaac would have very many descendants, like the stars of heaven.

3. God would bless all nations in the world through the Lord Jesus Christ, the great Descendant of Isaac, 26.4; 12.3. This is the way the Holy Spirit explained these verses in Galatians 3.8,16.

3/26 Isaac obeyed the Lord's command and stayed in the land of Palestine. However he was living among the Philistines and he was afraid that they would kill him to take his wife, 26.6-11. So he lied about Rebekah and said, "She is my sister." But Abimelech found out that Rebekah was Isaac's wife so he called Isaac and rebuked him. He also told his people not to touch Isaac or his wife.

Isaac was following the example of his father when he did these things. Abraham had lied about his wife both in Egypt and in the land of the Philistines, 12.13; 20.2. Abimelech king of Gerar had put Abraham to shame over 60 years before this time.

(Abimelech in chapter 26 may have been the son of the Abimelech in chapter 20). We have to say that Abraham gave his son a poor example by doing these things. However a wise man will learn lessons from the lives of others. Isaac should have learned from the life of his father, and we should learn lessons from the lives of Abraham, Isaac and Jacob.

3/27 Isaac stayed for a while in the land of the Philistines and planted food. He got a great crop and became richer than ever, and this made the Philistines jealous, 26.12-16. Years before this Abimelech had promised to be a friend of Abraham, 21.32, but now his men broke this promise by filling with earth the wells of water which Abraham's servants had dug. Abimelech suggested that Isaac should move away before there was any trouble.

This is the only place where we read that Abraham, Isaac or Jacob planted food. It was not God's will that they should settle down in the land of Canaan. At this time God wanted them to live in tents like strangers, 12.8; 13.3; Hebrews 11.9. We too should walk as strangers through this world, 1 Peter 2.11.

3/28 The Philistines did not make Isaac feel welcome, so Isaac went away and dug again other wells, 26.17-22. His men also dug two new wells but the Philistines quarreled about them. Isaac moved still further away and at last the Philistines left him alone.

Then Isaac went back to Beersheba and the Lord appeared to him the second time, 26.23-25. Isaac built an altar, put up his tent, and dug a well.

3/29 Then Abimelech came to Isaac in a friendly way and wanted to make an agreement with him, 26.26-33. The Philistine king said that his men had done no wrong to Isaac, 26.29, but this was not really true, 26.15,18,20,21. However they agreed that Jehovah was with Isaac, and Isaac himself wanted to live in peace. Isaac's servants found more water on the very day that the men went away.

The Lord Jesus taught that peacemakers shall be called the sons of God, Matthew 5.9. In this chapter we see Isaac the man of peace. His quiet way showed the men of the world that God was with him and God also was pleased. Isaac was a good example for us, 2 Timothy 2.24; Hebrews 12.14.

We have seen that Esau had no real desire in his heart for the things of the Lord. He took two wives when he was forty years old, and Isaac was 100. Both of these wives were Hittites who did not know the Lord.

This made Isaac and Rebekah very sorry, 26.34,35.

 No believer should marry an unbeliever, 2 Corinthians 6.14. You will be sorry if you do and also you will make the Lord sad.

Isaac blessed his two sons, chapter 27

3/30 Isaac became blind when he was old and thought he did not have much more time to live. He was 137 years old but he lived to be 180, 35.28. He wanted to give his special blessing to Esau. Isaac knew God's promise about Jacob: *the older shall serve the younger*, 25.23. Still he loved his older son Esau and was more interested in eating Esau's food than in doing the will of God. He called Esau and asked him to go out and kill a wild animal, then prepare some food, and Isaac would bless him, 27.1-4.

4/1 Rebekah heard these words and told Jacob, after Esau had gone out. She wanted Jacob to get the chief blessing, so she suggested that he should kill two young goats. Rebekah would prepare the meat so it would taste like wild meat. Then Jacob would take it in to Isaac and he would get the blessing, 27.5-17.

4/2 Jacob did not refuse this plan and was willing to deceive his father, but he was afraid he would get caught. Esau had a lot of hair on his skin, but Jacob had smooth skin. Jacob was afraid his father would touch him so he would know it was not Esau. This would bring on Jacob a curse and not a blessing. Rebekah said that she would take the curse, but of course Jacob was equally guilty. Just to be sure, Rebekah dressed Jacob in Esau's clothes and put the hairy skin of the goats on his hands and neck.

Some mothers teach their children the wrong way and they will be sorry for it. However Jacob was about 77 years old at this time. He should have refused his mother's advice and done what was right.

So Jacob went in with the meat and Isaac was surprised because he got it so soon, 27.18-29. Jacob said that the *Lord* had helped him. Isaac knew that it was Jacob's voice, but the hands felt like Esau's hands. Jacob lied again and said that he was really Esau. Isaac thought he would know him by the smell of the clothing, but Jacob was wearing Esau's clothes, 27.26,27. So at last Isaac blessed Jacob and said he would be lord over all his brothers. Isaac passed on to Jacob the blessing of Abraham: *a curse on every one who curses you and a blessing on every one who blesses you*, 27.29; 12.3.

It is a terrible thing to use the name of the true God while telling a lie, 27.20. Jacob also deceived his father with a kiss, 27.27. A kiss is a sign of love but there was no love in Jacob's heart for his father at this time. In this way he was like Judas, Luke 22.48.

4/3 Jacob left his father and Esau came in at once. This time Isaac knew the voice of Esau. He saw that he had made a great mistake and began to shake all over, but he knew that he could not change the blessing given to Jacob, 27.33. Esau with tears asked for a blessing also, 27.34; Hebrews 12.16,17, but Isaac told him that he must serve his brother, 27.37.

Isaac also said that Esau would live far from the good land, 27.39,40. He would "live by his sword" which means he would live by fighting and robbing other people. However at times he would get free from his brother's control. These things were fulfilled in the history of the people of Edom, the sons of Esau.

4/4 Esau had no real desire for the spiritual blessing, 25.33, but he hated Jacob because his father had given it to him, 27.41. Esau made a plan to kill Jacob as soon as their father was dead. Esau did not really believe that the promise was from God. Isaac promised Jacob that God would curse all who cursed Jacob, 27.29, but Esau was not afraid of this.

Rebekah knew that Jacob was in great danger, so she told him to go away from home. She was afraid that Esau would kill Jacob when their father died and she did not want to lose her husband and her beloved son in the same day, 27.42-45.

In chapters 22 and 24 Isaac is a wonderful picture of our Lord Jesus Christ. Isaac obeyed his father, was offered up as a sacrifice and received his bride, a picture of the Church. But when Isaac became older he seemed more interested in food than in the will of God. He was willing to sell the precious promises of God to his son for a meal. We have seen that Esau sold his blessing for a meal. Esau was interested only in the things of this world. Rebekah and Jacob had a *desire* for spiritual blessing but were willing to tell lies to get it.

The New Testament does not record the sins of Old Testament saints, so we read only that Isaac promised blessings for Jacob and Esau in the future, Hebrews 11.20. We know that God controls everything according to His own will. God's purpose was that the older son should serve the younger. We can be sure He will work out His own purposes today and in the future.

Now test yourself

1. Why does the Bible tell us more about Isaac and Jacob than it does about Ishmael and Esau? *Isaac + Jacob = men of faith.* ✓
   Ishmael + Esau = men of the world; no desire for spiritual things

2. Why did Isaac and Rebekah pray?
   Isaac - prayed for Rebekah to get pregnant. ✓

3. How do you know that Genesis 12.3 and 26.4 speak of our Lord Jesus Christ? *The descendant will bless all nations. Galatians 3:8,16 says this is Jesus.* ✓

4. Why didn't Abraham, Isaac and Jacob plant food every year in the land of Canaan? *God wanted them to be strangers in the land + camp in tents. He provided their needs.* ✓

5. In Genesis 27, who did what was right, Isaac, Rebekah, Jacob or Esau?

6. Which of these four people is marked in the New Testament as unrighteous? *Esau : Hebrews 12:16 (Esau never thinks about God).* ✓

Turn to page 115 to check your answers.

None! ✓ *Isaac : knew God's blessing was for Jacob but wanted to give it to Esau anyway.* ✓

Rebekah + Jacob : Willing to lie to get God's spiritual blessing ✓

Esau : angry so planned to kill brother Jacob even though God's blessing was on him ✓

Rebekah prayed to find out why she felt the babies struggling in her ✓

- 8 -

JACOB'S FAMILY
chapters 28-33

4/5 *We have seen that Isaac gave the chief blessing to Jacob. Isaac had not planned it that way, but God was in control. No doubt Isaac knew in his heart that this was God's will. The story goes right on.*

Jacob left home, 28.1-9

Isaac understood that the Savior of the world would be a descendant of Jacob, and for this reason Jacob should not marry a Canaanite girl. Rebekah said she was tired of Esau's Hittite wives but there was more to it than that; she was afraid for Jacob. For these reasons Isaac commanded Jacob to go back to Padan-aram and choose a wife from the family of Laban, 27.46 - 28.2.

Jacob obeyed his father and before he left, Isaac blessed him and asked God to give Jacob the blessing of Abraham, 28.3-5. This second blessing was richer and fuller than the first, 27.28,29. This shows that Isaac was no longer fighting against the will of God.

Esau also tried to please his father, 28.6-9. He saw that his Hittite wives were causing trouble, so he took another wife, a daughter of Ishmael. Esau was completely without spiritual wisdom.

Jacob's dream, 28.10-22

4/6 Jacob started on his long journey to Haran. One night it got dark before he could reach a village, so he slept in an open place. He laid his head on a stone and in the night he had a strange dream. He saw angels going up to heaven and coming down again, 28.10-12. Jehovah spoke to Jacob and said He was the God of Abraham and Isaac, and promised to give him the land of Canaan. Jacob would have many children who would live in the land, and the Lord would look after Jacob until He had fulfilled His promise, 28.13-15. When Jacob woke up he was afraid because God had spoken to him.

60

4/7 In the morning Jacob took the stone and poured oil on it. He called
the place Bethel, which means *the house of God.* Jacob promised to
worship Jehovah and to give back to Him one part in ten of all which he
received, 28.16-22. Jacob promised he would do these things *if* God
would look after him. God had already promised to take care of him, so
Jacob did not need to have any doubts about this. He should have agreed
to worship Jehovah just because He is God.

We have seen that Jacob made a bargain with his brother over
his spiritual blessing. Here he is trying to do the same thing with
God. He offered to worship God if God would look after him
and bring him back safely. Many people today try to work their
way to heaven. They offer to God their good works and think
that He will have to give them eternal life. This is worse than
what Jacob did.

Later on God commanded believers in Old Testament times
to give one tenth of all they received. As Christians we know
that *everything* belongs to the Lord. Only His grace has saved us
from the judgment of God. My time, my life, my money, all
belong to Him, Romans 12.1. Young Christians should learn to
give to the Lord a tenth of all they receive, but the true joy of
giving comes when we really commit *everything* to Him.

Jacob and his wives, chapter 29

4/8 At last Jacob came to the end of his long journey. He saw a well of
water and many sheep around it. The shepherds were waiting until
all the sheep came together. Then they would roll away the stone and the
sheep could have water to drink, 29.1-3. Jacob asked the shepherds if
they knew Laban, his mother's brother. Just then Rachel, Laban's daughter, came to the well, 29.4-8.

4/9 Jacob at once rolled away the stone without waiting for the other
shepherds. He kissed Rachel and told her who he was, 29.9-20.
Laban welcomed Jacob because he was a relative, and Jacob stayed with
Laban for a month. Then Jacob agreed to serve Laban seven years for
Rachel, his younger daughter. This did not seem long to Jacob.

4/10 When the seven years were completed Laban made a great wedding feast. That evening he took his older daughter Leah and gave
her to Jacob instead of Rachel. But Jacob did not know until the morning
that Laban had deceived him. Laban explained what he had done by saying that it was not their custom for the younger daughter to get married
before the older daughter. So Jacob had to serve another seven years for

Rachel, 29.21-30. Laban gave a servant girl to each of his daughters, Zilpah and Bilhah, 29.24,29.

About 100 years had passed since Laban had received Abraham's servant, 24.29,30. At first Laban welcomed Jacob also, but soon he was willing to cheat him. Laban may have told the truth in verse 26, but still it was not right for him to deceive Jacob about Rachel. On the other hand we see that Jacob is beginning to get back some of the evil things he had done to others. He had been quite willing to lie to his father and to cheat his brother and now these things are happening to him. *A man will reap exactly what he plants,* Galatians 6.7.

4/11 Jacob loved Rachel more than Leah but the Lord knew that Leah was not to blame for this. God therefore gave Leah the privilege of becoming the mother of Jacob's first four children, who were all boys. She gave each one a name according to her feelings at that time.

Reuben:	"See, a son"
Simeon:	"Hearing"
Levi:	"Joined"
Judah:	"Praise"

At first Leah was thinking of herself and her troubles but when the fourth son was born she just praised the Lord. These sons became the fathers or ancestors of four tribes in Israel, and the meaning of their names is important when we read the history of these tribes. Moses was born of the tribe of Levi, and the Levites were helpers in the tabernacle and the temple. King David belonged to the tribe of Judah, and our Lord Jesus Christ as a Man is a Descendant of David and Judah.

Jacob's other sons, chapter 30

4/12 Rachel saw that she had no children, so she gave her servant Bilhah to Jacob, 30.1-8. In doing this she followed the example of Sarah, the mother of Isaac, her husband's father, 16.2. It was right that Rachel would want to have children, but she should have been willing to wait for God's time. Bilhah, her servant, had two sons and Rachel called them:

Dan:	"Judging"
Naphtali:	"My struggle"

In the beginning God made one wife for Adam and it is certainly His will that a man should have only one wife. Many men in Old Testament days took more than one wife but this does not mean that it was God's will for them. Today a man with more than one wife can be saved if he believes in the Lord Jesus Christ, but he cannot serve as a leader in the church, 1 Timothy 3.2,12. Read again 29.31-34 and 30.1,8,15, and you will see that a man will have trouble if he has more than one wife in his home.

4/13 Leah saw that she was not having any more children, so she gave her servant girl to Jacob, 30.9-13. Zilpah had two sons and Leah called them:

Gad: "Fortune"
Asher: "Happy"

Next we see Rachel and Leah quarreling over their husband, 30.14-21. Reuben, Leah's son, found some plants growing in the open field. When anyone eats a *mandrake* it acts on the body like medicine. Rachel wanted these plants and agreed that Leah should have Jacob that night. So Leah had another son and later her sixth son and a daughter also were born. The names of the sons are:

Issachar: "Wages"
Zebulun: "Honored"

At last Rachel stopped fighting with her sister and started praying to the Lord. When a baby boy was born, Rachel gave thanks to God but asked Him for another son, 30.22-24. She called his name:

Joseph: "Adding"

Jacob was 91 years old when Joseph was born.

	Joseph's age	Jacob's age	Read Genesis
Beginning of seven years of plenty	30		41.29, 30,46
Beginning of seven years of famine	37		
Joseph arrived in Egypt two years later	39		45.11
Jacob's age at the time		130	47.9

So Jacob was 91 years older than Joseph, which means that Jacob was 91 years old when Joseph was born.

4/14 By this time Jacob had finished serving Laban fourteen years for his two daughters. Jacob wanted to go back to his own country, but Laban wanted him to stay and look after his sheep, 30.25-36. Laban had to agree that the Lord was with Jacob, 30.27, but Jacob's life was certainly not without blame. Jacob was willing to stay and look after Laban's sheep if he could also raise his own. They agreed that animals with spots would belong to Jacob and the rest would belong to Laban.

4/15 God had promised to bless Jacob and supply all his needs, but Jacob was not satisfied with this. He did not fully trust the Lord and wanted to make sure he would be rich. He was willing to use more tricks in order to get rich, 30.37-43. He got most of Laban's cattle and became very rich, but he also got a lot of trouble with it.

>   It is no wonder that the Holy Spirit warns us about money. Those who want to be rich fall into a trap, and the love of money is a source of all kinds of evil, 1 Timothy 6.9,10. The Lord Jesus Christ taught the same things, Luke 12.15. Greedy people want more than what they have and this may be as bad as worshiping idols, Colossians 3.5.

Jacob started back home, chapter 31

4/16 So Jacob became rich and this made the sons of Laban very jealous. They said that Jacob was taking their father's property, 31.1,2. Jacob called Rachel and Leah and told them that their father had changed his wages ten times. Jacob said that God had blessed him and given him the cattle of their father. Now God had appeared to him and told him to go back to his own land, 31.3-13.

>   It is hard to tell which of these two men, Jacob or Laban, was the worse. Neither was honest or fair with the other. Jacob said God had blessed him, but we know that God will not honor unfair and tricky actions.

4/17 Rachel and Leah did not really love their father and they were willing to go with Jacob to the land of Canaan, 31.14-16. They got ready to leave quickly and secretly. While Laban was away, Rachel stole some of his images. Rachel thought these images would bring her good luck, and this shows that she did not really believe in God. Jacob left with his whole family but did not even tell Laban that they were going, 31.17-21.

>   On the third day Laban heard that Jacob had run away. He and his men started after them, but God told Laban not to hurt Jacob, 31.22-24.

4/18 Laban asked Jacob why he had run away secretly; he said he would have liked to kiss his daughters and grandchildren good-bye. God had told him not to harm Jacob. But why had he stolen Laban's images? Jacob answered by saying that he did not know anything about the images. He told Laban he could kill the person who had stolen these images, 31.25-32.

Laban started to look for his images in all the tents. Rachel had hidden them and was sitting on them. She said that she was sick and so she could not stand up for her father, 31.33-35. Because of this trick Laban did not find his images.

4/19 Now it was Jacob's turn to use strong words. He told Laban to set before the others anything belonging to him which he found in Jacob's tents. Then he said in front of everybody that Laban had changed his wages ten times and had treated him badly in many ways. He was sure Laban wanted to take away everything, but God had warned Laban not to touch him, 31.36-42.

4/20 Laban could not deny these things. He knew that he would be hurting his own daughters and their children if he attacked Jacob. So instead he offered to make a covenant of peace with Jacob. Jacob set up a stone as a pillar, as he had done before, 28.18. The other men gathered many stones into a pile and both Laban and Jacob gave the place a name. Laban called on Jehovah to watch Jacob so he would not do any harm to his daughters, 31.43-50. Jacob and Laban also promised each other not to return to hurt the other person, 31.51-54. Jacob swore by the God of his father and offered a sacrifice. Early the next morning Laban went back home, 31.55.

We can see the character of both Jacob and Laban in these verses. Both were selfish and quite willing to tell lies for money. Laban was held back by a real fear of Jehovah and Jacob twice called God the FEAR of Isaac, 31.42,53. This means the God whom Isaac feared and worshiped.

We should fear God in the same way that a child fears his father, 1 Peter 2.17. This means that we should show proper respect for God. With perfect love we can put away fear, 1 John 4.18, but we should always be afraid of doing anything which would cause the Father sorrow. Jacob and Laban did many things in these chapters which must have caused Him sorrow.

Jacob prepared to meet Esau, chapter 32

4/21 Jacob and Laban made this covenant but it was only an agreement not to attack one another. At least Jacob could feel safer because no one would come after him from behind, so he started to prepare for an enemy before him, his brother Esau. Jacob was beginning to learn that evil will always come back on the one who did wrong and now he was afraid of what his brother might do to him. God gave Jacob a vision of angels which he said was God's army sent to protect him, and he called the place *two* armies. This shows that he was trusting in his own company of men as well as in the power of the angels of God, 32.1,2; he was not ready to trust God alone.

Then Jacob sent men to Esau to tell him that he had become rich and he would like to return to the land if Esau was willing. Note that Jacob called Esau *my lord* and himself *your servant*, 32.4. This shows that he did not believe God's promise, *The older shall serve the younger*, 25.23.

Jacob's men soon returned and told him that Esau was coming with 400 men to meet *him*. Jacob was very much afraid that Esau would kill him. He did not believe the Lord's promise which God had given when He commanded him to return to the land of Canaan, 31.3. Jacob divided all his company into two groups and hoped that Esau would not find and kill both of them, 32.6-8.

How often we are the same! We Christians sometimes worry because we do not carry everything to God in prayer.

4/22 Jacob had prayed but he was still afraid and still trusting in his own wisdom. He thought he would soften Esau's anger by giving him 580 animals. He sent these out in five groups, each one in the charge of a servant. Each servant was to tell Esau that the animals were a gift for him and that Jacob followed behind, 32.13-21.

4/23 Even then Jacob was still afraid. He sent his wives and children over the river Jabbok but he stayed behind, 32.22-32. Jacob had done everything he could think of to prepare for meeting his brother, but God had to prepare Jacob himself. Jacob thought he was struggling with a man but it was really the angel of God, Hosea 12.4. Jacob struggled all night, and when the morning was near the angel touched Jacob's leg so that he could never walk straight again. He would not be able to fight his brother nor even to run away from him, so he could only trust the Lord.

Still Jacob would not go without a blessing, so the Lord gave him a new name: Israel. In the rest of the Bible the Holy Spirit calls Jacob, the *natural man*, by his old name. *Israel* is used for the spiritual man who has learned his lessons from God. Jacob called the place Penuel which means *the face of God*.

The Lord touched Jacob on the thigh to teach him that he could be strong in the Lord only when he knew that he himself was weak. The people of Israel would not eat this part of any animal, 32.32. This should have made Jacob and his children remember God's great lesson: God alone gives a believer any victory, blessing, or success, which he ever gets.

Jacob met Esau, chapter 33

4/24 Jacob saw Esau coming with 400 men but he had been all night with God and now he was ready to go at the head of his family to meet Esau, 33.1-3.

He found that he did not need to be afraid. Esau was not angry; he ran to meet him and kissed him. Jacob brought his family to Esau, first the servants and their children, then Leah and Rachel and their children. Jacob explained that all the animals were a gift for Esau. This large gift of animals was not necessary and Esau said he had enough already. However Jacob really wanted Esau to take the gift and in the end Esau accepted it, 33.4-11.

4/25 Then Esau suggested that they should travel together; this may have been because he wanted to keep a watch on Jacob. Jacob did not want to be with his brother, so he said that the children and the young sheep could not travel very quickly, 33.12-14.

Esau offered to leave some men to look after Jacob but Jacob did not want this either, 33.15-17. At the end Esau started back to the district of Seir, and Jacob went to a place which he called Succoth. Jacob and Esau did not really love or trust each other, and they did not meet again until Isaac's death, perhaps twenty years later, 35.29.

Jacob stayed some time in Succoth, then crossed the river Jordan and reached the city of Shechem, 33.18-20. God had commanded him to return to his family, 31.3, but he took many years to reach them. God had saved Jacob from the power of Esau and he should have obeyed Him fully. Instead he bought some land and lived near the wicked city of Shechem. He built an altar for God, but God could not bless him until he obeyed. Jacob did not return to his father Isaac until he got to Hebron, 35.27.

Jacob had a certain amount of real faith but he did not trust God fully. Today many people truly believe in the Lord Jesus but are afraid to trust Him for the things of this life. We should pray about every problem and trust the Lord to supply our needs, to take care of our families and to make us a blessing to others.

Now test yourself

1. Show from Genesis 28 that Esau did not have any spiritual understanding. *Took another wife from Ishmael's family + thought this was acceptable.* ✓
2. How did Laban first cheat Jacob? *Gave Leah to Jacob instead of Rachel* ✓
3. Which of Leah's sons became the most famous? Which of Rachel's sons?
4. Why did Rachel steal her father's images? *For good Luck* ✓
5. Why was Jacob afraid of Esau? *Cheated his brother + knew Esau wanted to kill him* ✓
6. Jacob called Esau *my lord*, 32.18; 33.8; and he called himself Esau's *servant*, 32.20; 33.5. Why was this wrong? *Didn't believe God's promise that Esau would serve Jacob* ✓

Turn to page 116 to check your answers.

Leah: *Levi ⟹ Moses' ancestor line.*
Judah ⟹ Jesus' line ✓

Rachel: Joseph.
⇓ ✓
Great Egyptian Ruler.

- 9 -
JACOB IN THE LAND OF CANAAN
chapters 34-38

4/26 *Jacob knew that God had commanded Abraham to live in the land as a stranger. Jacob had heard the story of Lot who lived in Sodom and whose children grew up in that wicked city. Jacob did not learn these lessons; in fact, he was quite willing to live near a city of the Hivites. In chapter 34 Jacob had a great deal of trouble, partly the result of living in the world and partly the result of his own earlier acts.*

Dinah and Shechem, chapter 34

Jacob had more than one daughter, 37.35; 46.7, but Dinah was the only one whose name we know. She was only about fourteen years old at this time. Dinah was not happy staying at home with her family and she went out to visit the women of the country. Shechem, the prince's son, took Dinah and forced her into sin. Then Shechem wanted to marry the girl and he asked his father Hamor to talk to Jacob about it. Dinah's brothers heard what had happened and they were very angry, 34.1-7.

4/27 Hamor told Jacob's sons that Shechem wanted to marry their sister. He suggested that Jacob's family could live together with his people. They could give their daughters to the Hivite men and the Hivites would give their daughters to the sons of Jacob. There was room for everyone and Jacob's family could get rich, 34.8-10.

4/28 Shechem himself promised to give anything the brothers demanded for the girl, 34.11,12. The sons of Jacob were very angry at Shechem for stealing their sister but at first they acted as if they were friends. They said they would agree to Hamor's suggestion only if all the men of their city were circumcised, 34.13-17.

4/29 Hamor and Shechem were quite willing to do this. They talked to the men of the city and told them they would soon get all Jacob's wealth, 34.21-23. (They had told Jacob and his sons that *they* would get rich, v.10). So the men of the city agreed to be circumcised, 34.24.

4/30 On the third day after the circumcisions the men of the city were still unable to fight, so Simeon and Levi attacked the town and killed them all. They took Dinah out of Shechem's house and brought her back to her father. Joseph was only fourteen at this time, but the other eight brothers went back into the city to steal anything they could find, including the women and children, 34.27-29. Jacob did not say they had done wrong but he was afraid that the other people of the land would come and kill them all. Simeon and Levi said they had a perfect right to get vengeance for their sister, 34.31.

> Jacob had been willing to lie to his father Isaac. Now Jacob's sons acted on their own without asking their father and they brought the whole family into terrible danger. Jacob and each one of us must pay the price of our own sin.

Jacob at Bethel, 35.1-15

5/1 Earlier the Lord had made Jacob willing to return to the land of Canaan when He gave him trouble with Laban. At that time the God of Bethel told Jacob to return to the land of his family, 31.3, 13. Now Jacob had wanted to settle down at Shechem but God allowed trouble in his life to make him willing to obey. God commanded him to go to Bethel, 35.1.

Why Bethel? Remember that Abraham had a real experience with God in Bethel, 12.8; 13.3. God had also appeared to Jacob at the same place, 28.19, and now He wanted Jacob to go back there. Jacob was willing, but first he commanded his family and his servants to put away their idols. Rachel was not the only one who had brought gods from Padanaram. Jacob buried these idols under a tree, 35.2-4.

So they journeyed to Bethel and God made the men of the country afraid to attack Jacob. In this way Jacob arrived safely at Bethel and he built an altar as the Lord had commanded, 35.1,7.

> Jacob built his first altar in the wrong place and without God's command, 33.20. We should do good things only in the right way and at the right time. For this we need to know God's will and God's Word.

At Bethel one of the older women died and was buried under a tree. Her name was Deborah and she had been with Rebekah, Jacob's mother, when Rebekah left home, 24.59. We do not know when or why she came to join Jacob's company but they were sorry when she died, 35.8.

5/2   Then God appeared to Jacob the second time, 35.9. This was almost thirty years after He appeared to him in a dream when Jacob ran away from Esau, 28.13; 35.1. This time God told him again that his name would be Israel and that God's name was *El-Shaddai* or God Almighty. God had revealed himself by this name to Abraham, 17.1, and Isaac had told Jacob about it, 28.3. Then God told Jacob again that he would become a great nation and that God would give the land to his children, 35.9-12.

Jacob set up a pillar of stone and poured wine and oil on it. He had already set up a stone pillar at Bethel, 28.18, and another at Mizpah, 31.45. A little later he put up a fourth pillar, at Bethlehem, 35.20. Jacob set up these two stone pillars at Bethel to help him remember the place where God had appeared to him. This was good, but later Bethel became a place of sin for the people of Israel, Amos 4.4. Even good things may become evil if our hearts are not right with God.

Benjamin was born, 35.16-29

5/3   Years before, Rachel called her first son Joseph which means *Adding*. She was sure that God would give her another son, and fourteen years later God answered her prayer. Jacob and his family were traveling from Bethel to Bethlehem when Rachel began to have great pain. The woman who helped her thought that she would be all right and told her not to be afraid. The baby was born and lived, but the mother died.

Just before Rachel died she called the baby's name Ben-oni, which means *the son of my sorrow*. Jacob loved Rachel and was very sorry when she died, but he changed the baby's name to Benjamin, *the son of the right hand*. Jacob was 105 years old at this time and we will see that he loved Benjamin because this child was born when he was old, 44.20.

In these two names we see a picture of the Son of God. The Lord Jesus was *the man of sorrows*, Isaiah 53.3, like Ben-oni. He gave His life for us and rose again from death; then He sat down at God's *right hand* far above every name which is named, Ephesians 1.20,21, like Benjamin.

Jacob had still more trouble at this time. His oldest son Reuben fell into sin with Bilhah, one of Jacob's concubines. Jacob knew about this, 35.22, but did nothing to punish his son. He did remember it later on when he blessed his sons just before he died, 49.3,4.

5/4 By now Jacob had twelve sons. Their names are found in verses
23-26; also their mothers' names. These sons were all born in
Padan-aram except Benjamin; he alone was born in Canaan.

At last Jacob and his family came to Mamre where Isaac his father
was still living. Soon after that Isaac died at the age of 180. Esau and
Jacob buried him in the same place where Sarah, Abraham and Leah
were buried, 49.29-31, and later Jacob himself was buried there,
50.12,13.

The sons of Esau, chapter 36

5/5 Esau was a worldly man without any real desire for spiritual
blessing. We read six names of Esau's wives in Genesis 26.34; 28.9
and 36.2,3. However two of these may have had two names each so we
can say that Esau had between four and six wives. Esau had a large family and was very wealthy and he did not want to live near his brother
Jacob. He moved to the hill country of Seir which was south of the Dead
Sea. Seir was also called Edom because that was Esau's second name,
25.30; 36.1,8,9.

5/6 We read the names of Esau's sons and of their sons in verses 9 to
19. Then there is a list of important people, the sons of Seir, who
lived in the land before Esau moved there, 36.20-30. After that we have
a list of eight kings and eleven chiefs.

5/7 So the Bible gives only a short account of the life and history of
Esau, the son of Isaac, and then in chapter 37 we turn back to the
story of Jacob and his sons. You remember we saw a short account of
Ishmael's life in 25.12-18, but very much more about Isaac.

We can learn from this that the important people in the world
are those who obey God. Others may seem very wealthy and
receive great honor but the glory of this world does not last very
long. He who does the will of God lives for ever, 1 John 2.17.

Joseph was loved and hated, chapter 37

5/8 Jacob was 108 years old by now. He was living in the land which
God had promised to him, the land where Abraham and Isaac had
lived. Joseph becomes the most important person in the remaining chapters of Genesis, except chapter 38.

Joseph was now 17 years old and he helped his brothers look after
their father's sheep. His brothers were not behaving as they should and
Joseph told his father about it. In Ephesians 5.11 we are told to take no

part in the sins of others but instead we should bring them out to the light. Jacob loved Joseph more than his other sons and gave him a long coat to wear. This made his brothers hate him more than ever, 37.1-4.

There had been trouble in Jacob's family when *he* was young. His mother had shown special love to him but his father had loved his brother Esau. From this Jacob should have learned not to show special favor to any child in the family.

5/9 God honored Joseph because he did not follow the evil ways of his brothers and He planned a wonderful future for him. In those early days the Bible had not yet been written and God often spoke to men in dreams. He told Joseph in two dreams a little of His plans for him, 37.5-11. In the first dream the brothers were tying up grain in the field. Suddenly Joseph's grain stood up by itself and the grain of the others bowed down to his grain! The brothers understood this to mean that Joseph would rule over them.

In the second dream, the sun, moon and eleven stars all bowed down to Joseph. The eleven stars suggest Joseph's eleven brothers and the sun and the moon speak of his father and Leah. Even Jacob could not believe that he would bow down to his son, but he kept these things in his mind. The ten brothers hated Joseph all the more, 37.5,8, and were jealous of him, 37.11; Acts 7.9.

In these verses we see that Joseph's father loved him and that God loved him, but his brothers hated him. Joseph is a wonderful picture of our Lord Jesus Christ, the Son of God, whose Father always loved Him. He came into this world but His brothers in Israel hated Him. *He came to His own country and His own people did not receive Him,* John 1.11.

The Lord Jesus also rebuked men for their sins. He was doing His Father's will, but men hated Him all the more for rebuking them.

5/10 About this time Joseph's brothers took their father's sheep and cattle to feed them near the city of Shechem. They did not seem to care about the trouble and the danger they had seen at Shechem before, chapter 34. Jacob was worried about them and wondered how they were getting along. God had taken care of Jacob, 35.5, but Jacob knew that his sons were not trusting in the Lord at all. Jacob wanted to send Joseph to see if the brothers were safe, 37.12-14. Joseph remembered that his brothers hated him and he might have been afraid of what they would do to him when his father was not near. However he agreed to obey his father's command at once. This again reminds us of our Lord Jesus Christ who always did His Father's will.

So Jacob sent young Joseph from Hebron to Shechem. This is a journey of about fifty miles (80 km), and Joseph would need about three days to walk there. When he reached Shechem he found that the brothers had gone on to Dothan, about eighteen miles (30 km) farther. The brothers saw him coming and made fun of him and called him *this dreamer*. They planned to kill him and to tell Jacob that some wild animal had eaten him.

5/11 Joseph's oldest brother Reuben saved his life when he suggested that they should throw him into a dry pit instead, 37.15-24. Reuben had already been in trouble with his father and did not want to have any part in killing his brother. He really planned to deliver Joseph and take him back to his father.

The brothers hated the long coat which Jacob had given to Joseph. First they took off this coat which was the sign of the father's love, then they threw Joseph into the pit. Young Joseph begged them to let him out, as the brothers said later on, 42.21, but they just sat down and began to eat their food, 37.25.

Just at this time they saw some men on camels traveling on their way to Egypt. Judah was like Reuben, he did not want to kill Joseph. He suggested that they should sell Joseph as a slave, so they sold him for twenty pieces of silver, 37.26-28.

5/12 Reuben was not there at the time and when he returned he found that Joseph was not in the pit. Reuben was very sorry and did not know what to do, 37.29-36, but the brothers were not at all sorry. They just dipped Joseph's long coat in the blood of a goat and took it to Jacob. Jacob knew it was his son's coat and felt sure that a wild animal had killed him.

Jacob put rough sackcloth on his body and was full of sorrow for his son for many days. His family tried to comfort him but he said he would mourn for Joseph until the time of his death, 37.35. However, Joseph was really still alive and he was sold to Potiphar, an officer of the king of Egypt.

We will read more about Joseph in chapter 39, but first we have the sad story of Judah.

Again we see in this chapter that God is both good and righteous. God was good in looking after Joseph, and Joseph suffered only because of his wicked brothers. On the other hand

Jacob had lied to his father and now we see him again in great trouble because his sons lied to him. Later on we will see that God punished the brothers also for their sin.

Judah and his family, chapter 38

5/13 Judah was just as guilty as his brothers when they sold Joseph as a slave and lied to their father about him. Chapter 38 tells us the story of Judah's own sin. Years before this Judah had left his brothers and made friends with the people of Canaan, especially Hirah, a man of Adullam. Judah did not try to win the people of Canaan for the Lord, instead he followed their evil ways. We never hear of Hirah again, but later on David lived with his men in the cave of Adullam before he became king, 1 Samuel 22.1,2.

Judah soon married a girl of Canaan and after a time she had three sons. The oldest boy grew up and Judah took a wife for him, another Canaanite girl called Tamar. Judah's son lived a wicked life and the Lord put him to death, 38.1-7.

Judah knew that the blessing of Abraham and Isaac would be given to one of Jacob's sons. God had promised that the Savior of the world would be a descendant of Abraham, Isaac and Jacob, and Judah understood that it was important that the family line should be continued. So he gave his son's wife to his second son Onan. Later this practice became a law, Deuteronomy 25.5-10; Matthew 22.24.

Onan would not agree to this law and he died also as a sinner. Judah's third son was not yet grown and so Judah told Tamar to go back to her father's house for a while, 38.8-11. Really Judah was afraid that his third son would die also.

Judah did wrong when he left his brothers and his father's family and went to make friends with the people of this world. This was the first step in Judah's downfall. He knew the story of Esau and he should have understood that it was wrong to marry a Canaanite girl. Two of his sons died because of their sin but Judah would not take the warning, nor believe that God was speaking to him. Instead he thought that Tamar was to blame; he deceived her and sent her away.

5/14 Joseph was in Egypt and away from his father about twenty years in all. During this time Judah's two sons died and at last his wife died also, 38.12-19. Then Judah fell into more sin.

It was at the time when people cut the wool from the sheep. This is done once or twice a year and is often a time of feasting and drinking, 1 Samuel 25.4,36; 2 Samuel 13.23,24.

Tamar knew Judah had lied to her and thought this was a good time to pay him back. She saw that her husband's brother was grown up but she was not given to him, so she dressed up like an evil woman and sat down beside the road. Judah did not know who she was and he promised to pay her the price of sin. He gave her three things to keep until he paid her.

5/15 Judah sent his friend Hirah with an animal to pay the woman. The people of that place did not know what had happened and Tamar wanted to keep the three things which Judah had given her, 38.20-23. So Hirah returned to Judah and said he could not find the woman.

After a few months everybody could see that Tamar was going to have a baby. Judah said that she had fallen into sin and must be put to death. Tamar answered that the father of the baby had given her these three things. When Judah saw them he agreed that the child was his, 38.24-26.

5/16 When the time came Tamar gave birth to two baby boys. It was important to know which one was born first, so the woman who helped Tamar put a piece of string around the finger of the first baby. The two boys were called Zerah and Perez, 38.27-30.

Judah accepted these two boys as his sons and returned to live with his father. He showed by his life that he was really sorry for his sin, and later on Jacob gave him the place of honor in the family. We do not hear of Judah's third son, Shelah, 38.5, again; the family's blessing went to Perez. You might think that Zerah, the first baby, should have a special blessing, but we have seen that God does not always choose the firstborn.

Here is the great lesson of this chapter: God will not let His children go on in sin; instead, He plans things to bring them back to Himself. We might fall into terrible sin but God is watching us and wants us to return. Judah was away from home and away from the Lord. Tamar was equally guilty, but the Lord used this sin to bring Judah back to Himself. As Christians we should give the Lord the chief place in our lives; if not we will fall into sin and shame. If we truly repent, God is able to forgive us and bring us back to the place of blessing.

The Lord Jesus Christ was born a descendant of Judah and of Perez,

Matthew 1.3. Does this mean that God honors the shameful, sinful act of Judah in this chapter? No, it means that God's grace is greater than any sin. *Where sin increased, God's grace increased much more*, Romans 5.20.

God can always gain the victory over sin, but He will do so only if the sinner is ready to repent and do the will of God.

In chapter 37 we saw that Joseph was a picture of Christ, because he was rejected by his brothers. Now we will read chapter 39 and learn how Joseph began to receive great glory. The sad story of Judah is in chapter 38, and it suggests the history of the Jews, who are the descendants of Judah. They turned against the Lord Jesus many years ago, and the time of Christ's glory is still in the future. In the years between, the Jews have fallen into great sin and suffer many troubles. We know from Romans 11 and other scriptures that Israel will repent of their sins, like Judah, and will be restored to the favor of the Lord.

Chapter		
37	Joseph, a picture of the Lord Jesus Christ when He was rejected.	Past
38	Judah, a picture of the Jews in sin and in great trouble.	Present
39	Joseph glorified, a picture of our Lord.	Future

Now test yourself

1. Why did Jacob's sons lie to Hamor and Shechem? *Deceived them to think they were friends to attack + get revenge for Dinah*
2. What did God call Himself when He appeared to Jacob the second time? *El-Shaddai (almighty God)* ✓
3. Show that Benjamin is a picture of Christ. *First called Ben-Oni (son of my sorrow), then Benjamin & we think of* *
4. Why does the Bible give so little space to the family of Esau? *He was not man of God + descendants worldly men*
5. How was Joseph a picture of Christ in chapter 37?
6. How many sons did Judah have? Which one became the ancestor of the Lord Jesus Christ? *5 ; Perez* ✓✓

Turn to page 116 to check your answers.

* *Christ at God's right hand.*

Both hated by brothers but loved by Father. Both rebuked brothers (for sins) + were hated for it. ✓

- 10 -

JOSEPH'S TROUBLE AND GLORY
chapters 39 – 45

5/17 Joseph is the main character in the rest of the book of Genesis, but Jacob is seen a few times and we do not read of his death until chapter 49. What kind of a man was Jacob? Jacob had a true desire for spiritual blessing but he could not trust God to fulfill His promises. Before Jacob was born God had promised, "The older son shall serve the younger." Jacob was willing to use any means to gain his own purposes and so he was no better than men of this world. Jacob was willing to lie to get the blessing. He deceived Isaac his father, and Laban, the father of his two wives, chapters 27, 30.

Jacob reaped what he sowed and more of it. A man puts seed in the ground and he gets the same kind of food as he planted but much more of it. What did Jacob reap?

1. Laban deceived Jacob about Rachel, and Jacob had to work another seven years for the wife he loved, chapter 29.

2. Rachel deceived Jacob about the images which she had stolen from her father, chapter 31.

3. Jacob's ten sons deceived him cruelly about Joseph, chapter 37.

Does it seem strange to you that anyone would seek spiritual blessing by worldly means? Yet there are thousands of people who try to earn salvation by good works. They think that they must do many good things and hope that perhaps God will forgive them for their sins. They forget that God desires to bless sinners and to save them if they will repent.

Other people act as if they had no sin. It is not possible to deceive God, so there is no need to try. God wants to forgive your sins. If God forgives you, you may not have to reap the evil which you have sown. The Lord Jesus died for those sins; He reaped what He did *not* sow.

79

God forgives our sins and we are His children by faith, but He will teach us necessary lessons if we fall into sin. You must repent, or the hand of the Lord will be heavy upon you. God will not take away the gift of eternal life. He will never put a true believer into the lake of fire. But God as Father will teach him his lessons unless he confesses his wrong and stops sinning.

Joseph's trouble in Egypt, chapter 39

The Bible tells the story of many good men but we do not read in the Old Testament about anyone who was sinless or perfect. We know that all have sinned and the Lord Jesus Christ is the only perfect Man. The Holy Spirit gives many chapters in Genesis to the story of Joseph and we do not see any great sins of Joseph in this record. We have already seen in chapter 37 that Joseph stood up for what was right and would not go along with his brothers in their evil ways. He obeyed his father's will even when it meant going to a dangerous place. Joseph is a wonderful picture of our Lord Jesus.

Joseph's brothers sold him as a slave to the Ishmaelites and they sold him in Egypt to Potiphar who was an officer of Pharaoh. Joseph was just a slave to Potiphar, but the Lord was with him and blessed all he did. When Potiphar saw this, he made Joseph a ruler over his house. So the Lord kept on blessing Joseph and the house of Potiphar. After a while Joseph became the head over all Potiphar's servants, 39.1-6.

5/18   We must be on guard against Satan especially when things are going well, because it is just at this time that he tries to tempt us. In Joseph's case Potiphar's wife tried to lead him into sin. Joseph refused to sin against God but this woman would not leave him alone. At last she seized Joseph's clothing but he ran out of the house and left his coat with her. The woman told everybody that Joseph had tried to attack her but he had run away when she cried out, 39.7-17.

5/19   Potiphar became very angry and put Joseph in prison, 39.19-23, but even there the Lord was with Joseph, and the prison guard put the other prisoners in Joseph's care.

Joseph could have saved himself a lot of trouble by doing what the woman wanted, but he knew that this would be a terrible sin against God. He also was sure that God would know all about it. Joseph had more peace in his heart while in prison than if he had sinned in Potiphar's house. It is better to suffer for the right than to enjoy the pleasure of sin.

Pharaoh's two servants and their dreams, chapter 40

5/20 In old times God often spoke to men by dreams. We have read about Joseph's two dreams in 37.5-11. Now two of Pharaoh's servants had dreams in the same night.

Important people are often in danger because someone may try to kill them. This was also true in the time of Joseph. Pharaoh wanted to be sure that no one would put poison in his food or drink, and his butler and baker were expected to look after these things. But Pharaoh got sick and thought that someone had tried to poison him, so he put both the butler and the baker into prison. The guard of the prison told Joseph to look after them.

One night each of these men had a dream and neither one of them could understand the meaning of the dream. Joseph was a man of God and he told them that God would help him to understand.

5/21 In his dream the butler saw himself looking after Pharaoh in the way he should. Joseph said that this meant Pharaoh would give
5/22 the chief butler his old place, 40.9-15. In the chief baker's dream he allowed the birds to come and eat Pharaoh's food. This dream meant that the chief baker was the guilty one and Joseph told him that Pharaoh would put him to death in three days, 40.16-19.

Three days later Pharaoh did what Joseph had said. It was his birthday and he gave a big feast for all his servants. The chief butler was back at his old work looking after Pharaoh, but the chief baker had to die.

The chief butler had been wrongly put into prison, as Joseph had been. You might think that the butler would remember Joseph and ask Pharaoh to help him. Joseph had requested him to do this, 40.14,15, but the chief butler forgot all about it, 40.23.

Many people of this world do not remember those who have been kind to them, or tried to help them. In fact millions of people never even give thanks to God for all His goodness, Romans 1.21.

Joseph was left in prison for many more months because God had other lessons for him to learn. Perhaps Joseph should have been willing to wait for God's time instead of asking the butler, a man of this world, to help him. This might seem to be the only mistake that Joseph made. If so, let us always remember to wait for God's time and not take things into our own hands. Joseph knew the mind of God and could explain the meaning of the two dreams but still he

Conjecture – no biblical evidence for this.

had to learn for himself to wait until God's time would come.

Joseph's glory in Egypt, chapter 41

5/23 God had shown Joseph by dreams that he would be glorified, 37.5,9. Joseph gained the victory when Potiphar's wife tried to lead him into sin, but he asked a man to help him get out of prison instead of waiting for God's time. God still had lessons for Joseph to learn and he stayed in prison for two more years.

You can understand the main lessons of Joseph's life by thinking of three words: beloved, hated, exalted.* Joseph was *beloved* when he was in his father's house. There he had two dreams, about the grain and the stars, sun and moon. Joseph's brothers *hated* him and so did Potiphar's wife. Joseph was put in prison and Pharaoh's two servants had dreams telling that one would die and one would be given his place again. God had a plan for Joseph and it was now time for God to give him *glory*, but first He gave Pharaoh two dreams.

In Pharaoh's first dream seven good fat cows came up out of the Nile river and started eating grass. Pharaoh watched them in his dream and he saw seven other cows come up out of the river. They were poor and thin and in the dream the poor thin cows ate up the fat ones, 41.2-4.

In the second dream Pharaoh saw seven ears of good grain on one plant, then he saw seven thin ears of grain appear and they ate up the seven good ears of grain. In the morning Pharaoh called for his wise men to explain the dream to him but they were not able to do so, 41.5-8.

5/24 Suddenly the chief butler remembered what Joseph had done for him. He told Pharaoh that a young Hebrew man had explained his dream to him while he was in prison, 41.9-13.

5/25 Pharaoh called for Joseph, and Joseph quickly got ready to stand before the king. He told Pharaoh that he was no wiser than other people but that God would help him to understand the dream.

5/26 Pharaoh told Joseph just what he had seen in his sleep, 41.14-24. Joseph saw at once that both dreams had the same meaning. God was kind to Pharaoh and had shown him what He was about to do. There would be plenty of food in Egypt for seven years, but after that there would be a time of great hunger for seven more years, 41.25-36. God had given Pharaoh two dreams with the same meaning to

* F.B. Meyer

show that He would certainly do these things in the near future.

5/27 Pharaoh had not asked Joseph to suggest what he should do but Joseph offered him a plan. Pharaoh should choose a wise man and set him over the people of Egypt. There would be plenty of food for seven years and this man should put one part out of five parts in store houses and save it for the years to come. Later the farms of Egypt would not supply enough food for the people but they would be able to eat what had been saved up from earlier years.

Pharaoh saw at once that this was a good idea. He understood that the Spirit of God was in Joseph and that Joseph could do this work better than anyone in Egypt. He made Joseph ruler over his house and over all the people of the land. Only Pharaoh himself would be greater than Joseph, 41.37-40.

Think of how Joseph felt at this minute! He could not believe what he heard and could not answer Pharaoh even one word. Pharaoh put a ring on Joseph's hand and dressed him in fine clothes to prove that it was true. Joseph rode through the streets of the city and all the people bowed before him. Pharaoh gave him authority over all the Egyptians, 41.44. He also gave him a new name and an Egyptian wife, 41.45.

So we see Joseph at the age of thirty, the ruler over all the land of Egypt, 41.46. God gave him this great glory as He had promised, and we will soon see Joseph's family bowing down to him also. We can always be sure that God will fulfill His promises but it may take a long time.

5/28 Things turned out just as Joseph had said. For seven years there was plenty of food and Joseph stored up a great deal of it in every city, 41.46-49.

During these years his wife had two sons. Joseph called the first one Manasseh because God caused him to *forget* all his troubles. Joseph called the second boy Ephraim because God was making him *fruitful* in saving the lives of many people.

God wants us to forget things which happened long ago and press forward, Philippians 3.13. We should remain in Christ and we too will become fruitful, John 15.5.

Soon the seven years were over and the people did not have enough food to eat. They asked Pharaoh for bread but he just told them to go to Joseph and do whatever he said, 41.55. Joseph sold food to the people of Egypt and to men who came from other countries as well, 41.56,57.

In the story of Joseph we see a beautiful picture of the Lord Jesus Christ. Often the Holy Spirit speaks of Christ in a hidden way in the Old Testament. We love the Lord Jesus and we are happy to find many little suggestions which make us think of our wonderful Savior.

1. The Lord Jesus was beloved by God His Father, but He was hated by His brothers as well as by the men of this world.

2. Joseph was in prison, in the place of death, and he might have died there. He was brought out of prison *and* given glory. God not only raised the Lord Jesus from death, He also made Him to sit at His right hand, Ephesians 1.20.

3. Joseph is the first person in the Bible of whom it is said that the Spirit of God was in him, 41.38. God gave to Christ the fullness of the Spirit, John 3.34.

4. Joseph was a very wise man, but all the treasures of wisdom and knowledge are in Christ, Colossians 2.3. Joseph became ruler over all the land of Egypt but was still under Pharaoh the king. So we read that God will put all things under Christ, but the Son will be subject to God and God will rule over all, 1 Corinthians 15.25-28.

5. We do not know what Joseph's new name, Zaphnath-Paaneah, means, but some people think it may mean *The one who reveals secrets* or *savior of the world*. The Lord Jesus Christ was both. In John 4 He could reveal the secrets of the heart, verse 29; He was also the Savior of men, v.42.

6. Joseph got a Gentile girl for his wife. The Lord Jesus will receive the Church as His Bride after His time of waiting is over. The Church is neither Jewish nor Gentile, but most Christians are Gentiles by nature.

7. Pharaoh told the people to do just what Joseph said, 41.55, and the disciples of Christ should obey every command of His, John 14.23.

We have noticed that dreams were important in the changing periods of Joseph's life.

We may also think of four different kinds of clothing which he wore. When Joseph was beloved he wore a long coat which his father had given him. This coat was dipped in blood, 37.31.

When Joseph was hated he wore the clothing of a servant. The wicked woman seized this clothing and accused Joseph of trying to sin with her, 39.12.

Then he wore the clothing of a prisoner. He put this aside when the time of his suffering was over, 41.14.

Then Joseph was given a place of great honor and wore the clothing of the king, 41.42.

What lesson can we learn from this part of Joseph's life? We must learn to wait for God's good time and believe His promises. God is in control of everything and He works all things together for good according to His plan.

JOSEPH WAS EXALTED AMONG HIS BROTHERS
chapters 42-45

5/29 The people of Israel are by nature the brothers of the Lord Jesus Christ because the Lord was born into the nation of Israel. Israel hated Him and put Him to death, but the Bible tells us that they will be brought back to Christ in the future. The next few chapters in Genesis show us how Joseph brought his brothers to the place where they were willing to repent of the evil they had done to him; then Joseph gladly forgave them.

The first visit to Egypt, chapter 42

In Canaan the supply of food was getting low and Jacob heard that there was grain in Egypt, 42.1-4. He told his sons to go to buy some food but they were not happy about this. Jacob did not know that they had sold Joseph into Egypt as a slave. He said to them, "Why are you looking at one another?" His sons agreed to go but Jacob kept Benjamin safely at home.

5/30 The brothers arrived in Egypt and Joseph knew at once who they were. They had not seen him for twenty years and, of course, never expected that he would be the ruler of the land, 42.5-17. Joseph did not tell them at first who he was but spoke roughly to them. They bowed before him and he remembered his dreams and wondered if they felt sorry for their sin.

Joseph said the brothers must be enemies who had come to look over the land. They denied this sin and said they were ten of the twelve sons of one man. Joseph said they could prove it by sending one of them to bring back the youngest brother. The men knew that this would make Jacob very unhappy and they wished they had not told Joseph about their younger brother. Then Joseph put them all in prison for three days so they would learn what it felt like to be in prison.

6/1 After that Joseph told them that they could go back home but he would keep one of them. The brothers knew by now that they were in trouble and spoke among themselves in the Hebrew language, 42.18-25. Of course Joseph understood them and he noted that they were beginning to feel sorry for their sin against him. Joseph tied up Simeon and put the money they had paid for their food back into the bags of grain.

The nine men started back home to Jacob. On the way home, one of them found his money in his bag and they were all afraid that Joseph would blame them for stealing the money again. They began to see that God was punishing them for what they had done.

Why did Joseph put the money back into the bags of grain? He wanted his brothers to know what it means to be falsely accused. Here and in chapter 43 Joseph was trying to reach into the hearts of his brothers. A man must really repent for his sin or he will never know the peace of forgiveness.

6/2 The nine brothers got back to Jacob and told him what had happened. They brought back food but everybody knew it would not last very long. They could not get more food unless they took Benjamin back to Egypt. This was very bad news for their father Jacob, 42.29-34.

Then they emptied the bags of grain and every man was surprised to find his money back again. Jacob thought both Joseph and Simeon were lost and now they wanted to take Benjamin also! Reuben offered to give Jacob his two sons if he did not bring back Benjamin, but Jacob refused. Jacob thought he would die if anything happened to Benjamin.

Second visit to Egypt, chapter 43

6/3 Soon all the food was finished and Jacob told his sons to go to Egypt and get some more. They agreed to go, but only if Benjamin went with them. Judah said, "I will be *surety* for him." This meant that Judah promised to look after Benjamin and bring him back. Judah would be guilty if anything happened to his young brother. Jacob could trust Judah more than Reuben, 42.37, and so he finally accepted Judah's offer, 43.1-10.

6/4 Jacob told his sons to take some valuable gifts of food for the ruler of Egypt. They also took enough money to pay for the food they had bought on the first visit, 43.11-15. Jacob knew he also had to trust the Lord, 43.14.

Many years later the apostle Paul became *surety* for Onesimus, the slave who had run away from his master. Paul wrote to Philemon and said, *If Onesimus owes you anything, charge it to my account, I will pay you back*, Philemon 18,19. Judah and Paul are both beautiful pictures of our Lord Jesus Christ. The Lord became *surety* for our sins and paid the debt though we were far from Him. Any man may be very sorry if he agrees to pay the debt of a stranger, Proverbs 11.15. Our Lord Jesus Christ knew quite well what it would cost Him. We were far from God but He paid the price of our redemption on Calvary's cross.

6/5   The brothers arrived again in Egypt and they were taken right to Joseph's house. They were afraid that they would be punished for not paying for the grain the first time. They tried to explain to Joseph's servant, but he told them not to worry. They got their present ready to give to Joseph, 43.16-25.

6/6   Joseph came in and asked if their father was well. Then he saw his own brother Benjamin, the son of his mother, and he could hardly control himself, 43.26-34. The brothers had brought their special gifts for Joseph, 43.11, but we do not read that he accepted them. He was only interested in seeing Benjamin, the son of the father's right hand.

Then the servants brought food and the brothers ate separately from Joseph. They were greatly surprised to find they were seated in the right order according to their ages. Benjamin was given five times as much as any of the rest. This was another test to see if the brothers would be jealous of him.

Men are always trying to bring their gifts to God because they hope that He will forgive them. God's only question is: Do you have Christ? *He who has the Son has life indeed but he who has not the Son of God has not that life,* 1 John 5.12. Joseph's brothers would not have seen him, even though they had brought great gifts, if they had not brought the son. Have you received the Lord Jesus Christ as your Savior?

The brothers confessed their sins, chapter 44

6/7   Some people want to look important, so they say that they can *divine* or tell about future things. Joseph was able to tell the future but he knew that God gave him this power, 41.16. Joseph had a silver cup but he did not use it to get special knowledge from spirits as the priests of Egypt did. He put his cup in Benjamin's bag as a last step to test the brothers and this really made them willing to repent.

Joseph also put the money in every man's bag and early the next morning the brothers started their journey back to Canaan, 44.1-5. Joseph quickly sent his servant after them.

6/8   The servant asked the brothers why they had stolen Joseph's silver cup. They denied everything and agreed that the guilty man should die. The cup was found in Benjamin's bag and they all went back to the city, feeling very worried, 44.6-13.

6/9   The brothers fell down before Joseph and Judah spoke for them all. He said they would all be Joseph's slaves but Joseph said that only the guilty one would be his slave, 44.14-17. Benjamin must stay but the others could go back home.

6/10   Judah knew how Jacob would feel about this and he told Joseph the whole story, 44.18-34. Benjamin was born to Jacob when he was old and so his father loved him especially. Judah was afraid that Jacob would die of sorrow if Benjamin did not return, so he asked if *he* could stay as Joseph's slave instead of Benjamin. In this way Judah fulfilled his promise to be surety for Benjamin, 43.9.

Joseph revealed himself to his brothers, chapter 45

6/11   Joseph now knew that his brothers had really repented. He could hardly control his feelings and so he ordered all the Egyptians to leave the room. Then Joseph spoke to his brothers in the Hebrew language and told them, "I am Joseph." But at first his brothers were so worried that they were afraid to answer him, 45.1-3.

6/12   Joseph explained to them that God had been in control of all things and Pharaoh had made him ruler over all the land of Egypt. There would still be five more years of famine and the brothers should tell Jacob to come down to Egypt. Then Joseph kissed Benjamin and all the brothers, 45.4-15.

The brothers knew they were guilty and had sinned against Joseph. No wonder they were afraid until they saw that Joseph really loved them! Many men know they are sinners and are afraid of God. They find it hard to believe that God can love them and forgive them without paying money or doing good works. God has proven His love to us by giving His Son to die. When we believe this, we will no longer be afraid of God and we will begin to love Him. Perfect love puts away all fear, 1 John 4.18.

6/13   Pharaoh and his servants soon heard about Joseph's brothers and they were very happy, 45.16-20. Pharaoh told Joseph to send his brothers back to get their families. He gave them wagons, and animals to pull them. This would save the women and children from walking all the way from Canaan. They would not have to bring all their goods because there would be plenty of everything in Egypt.

Joseph gave gifts to his brothers and his father, and told his brothers not to quarrel on the way back. He gave Benjamin some money and five times as much clothing as he gave to the others. He did not want his brothers to be jealous of Benjamin as they had been of him, 45.21-24.

Jacob had sent gifts to Joseph but Joseph was interested only in seeing his brother. Joseph sent far greater gifts back to his father. In the same way God is the One who gives gifts and pours out His blessings on those who believe on His Son. We can give to God but He will give far more to us.

The brothers got back home but Jacob could not believe that Joseph was alive and ruler over Egypt. Jacob knew his sons had told him lies before this. They told him the whole story and showed him the things from Joseph and at last Jacob believed and agreed to go to see his son, 45.25-28.

Jacob's sons told him that Joseph was alive *and* that he was ruler of all the land of Egypt. It would have been easy for Jacob to believe the first part, that Joseph was alive. It was more wonderful and harder to believe that he was ruler over all Egypt. These two things are true of our Lord Jesus Christ. God raised Him from death *and* gave Him glory at His own right side. We should praise God because the Lord Jesus now has great glory and we should tell others about it too.

Now test yourself

1. What did Jacob sow and reap? *He lied to his father + his sons lied to him*

2. Who loved Joseph? Who hated him? Who exalted him?
Father loved him ; Brothers hated him + woman in Egypt ; Pharoah exalted him + later his brothers + God .

3. Name three kinds of clothing which Joseph wore. *Long sleeved robe ; Servants clothes ; prison clothes.*

4. Why did Joseph put the money and the silver cup into the bags of food? *Wanted brothers to confess sins to him .*

5. Why did Joseph pay no attention to the valuable gifts which his brothers brought? *Only interested in Benjamin .*

6. Show how Joseph is a picture of Christ.

Now turn to page 116 to check your answers.

Both loved by father but hated by brothers.
Both given glory + brothers will bow to them.

- 11 -

JOSEPH AND HIS FAMILY
chapters 46-50

6/14 *We have seen that Joseph for a time was hated and rejected.
When this time was over he received great glory in the land of
Egypt. We have also seen how wisely he got his brothers to repent and in
the end they really believed that Joseph loved them and had forgiven
them. The remaining chapters of Genesis tell us about Joseph again living near his father and brothers.*

Jacob came to Egypt, chapters 46, 47

Jacob had good reasons to go to Egypt, but he wanted to be sure that
it was the Lord's will. God had told Abraham that his descendants would
be strangers in a strange land, 15.13. God's words to Abraham would
make Jacob more sure that he should go to Egypt. However Abraham
had a lot of trouble there, 12.19, and God had commanded Isaac in time of
famine not to go to Egypt, 26.2.

Jacob went first to Beersheba and offered sacrifices. There God
spoke to him again and told him to go to Egypt, 46.1-7. God promised
Jacob that he would see Joseph, and Jacob's descendants would become
a great nation and return some day to Canaan.

6/15 Jacob was now 130 years old, 47.28. He had many children and
their children had many more. Some of their names are given in
46.8-27. There may have been more, but there were 66 people who were
born to Jacob in the lands of Padan-Aram and Canaan, 46.26. Joseph and
his two sons were already in Egypt, and Jacob himself made the full
number of seventy, 46.27. However in Acts 7.14 we see that there were
75 in Jacob's family who came to Egypt, so there may have been eight
wives of Jacob's sons.

6/16 At last Jacob arrived in Goshen, which is the northeast part of the
land of Egypt, 46.28-34. Joseph went to Goshen to meet his father.

He told his brothers to tell Pharaoh that they were keepers of sheep and cattle.

Think of the joy in the hearts of both Joseph and Jacob when they met again after twenty years! This is a picture of the joy of the Lord Jesus Christ and His Father when the Lord went back to heaven. The Lord Jesus told His disciples, *If you love me you will be glad that I am going to the Father*, John 14.28. He said this because *He* was very glad. Joseph threw his arms around his father and wept with tears for a good while, 46.29.

Joseph was ruler over all the land of Egypt, but his brothers were not really welcome there because they were shepherds, 46.34. In the Bible Egypt is a picture of the world and the people of God are never really wanted. The Good Shepherd is still not welcome in this world.

6/17   Joseph explained to Pharaoh that his brothers were shepherds, and Pharaoh commanded that some of them should look after his cattle and sheep as well, 47.1-6.

6/18   Then Joseph brought his father in before Pharaoh, 47.7-12. Pharaoh asked Jacob, "How old are you?" Jacob said he was 130 years old but he had seen a great deal of trouble. His father and grandfather had lived to greater ages. (Isaac was 180 when he died, Abraham 175.) As a man Jacob confessed that he had seen a lot of trouble, but he was a saint of God and a prophet and he could bless the king of Egypt, 47.10. Joseph gave his family a place to live in the district of Rameses in the land of Goshen, in the northeast part of Egypt.

We still have the old sinful nature in us, and even as Christians, we are far from being perfect. However we can ask God to bless people and God will answer prayer in the name of His Son.

6/19   Joseph was the governor of the land of Egypt and he sold food to the people. When their money was all gone they gave Pharaoh their cattle and sheep, 47.13-17, to obtain enough food for another year.

6/20   When this food was finished too, the people told Joseph that they would sell Pharaoh their land for more food and they themselves would be slaves of Pharaoh, 47.18-26. In this way Pharaoh gained complete control over all the land and the people of Egypt. Joseph made them promise to give the fifth part of all their crops to Pharaoh at harvest time. However before this Pharaoh had promised to give food to the priests and so they kept their own land.

The people thought that Joseph had saved their lives and they were willing to become Pharaoh's slaves. For us it is the Lord Jesus Christ who has saved our lives and we are happy to give Him all we have. We should offer our bodies as a living sacrifice to God, Romans 12.1, and use our bodies only for God's glory, 1 Corinthians 6.20.

The sons of Israel settled in the land of Goshen and became rich and had many children. Jacob was coming to the end of his life but he had lived in Egypt for seventeen years, 47.27,28. He made Joseph promise to bury him in the land of Canaan, 47.29-31.

Jacob blessed the sons of Joseph, chapter 48

6/21   Joseph heard that Jacob was sick and he went to see him with his two sons Manasseh and Ephraim. Jacob told Joseph about God's promise to make his descendants into a great nation, and to give them the land of Canaan. Jacob took Ephraim and Manasseh as his own sons, 48.1-7. Joseph was the first son born to Rachel, Jacob's beloved wife, and Jacob chose Joseph as his firstborn. This meant that he would get twice as much of the father's property as any other son. For this reason Joseph's two sons would each get as much as any other son of Jacob.

6/22   Jacob was very old and almost blind. Joseph brought his two sons to Jacob and Jacob gave thanks to God. Previously he thought that Joseph had been killed by an animal, but now he thanked God for seeing not only Joseph but his two sons as well.

Joseph presented Manasseh to Jacob so that Manasseh would be at Jacob's right hand and Ephraim at his left. This was so that Manasseh, the older boy, would get the chief blessing. Jacob gave them both a blessing, but he crossed his hands so that his right hand was on the head 6/23   of Ephraim, 48.8-16. Jacob knew that God wanted to give the chief blessing to the younger son, and so here he was more spiritual than his father Isaac when he blessed his two sons, chapter 27. Joseph thought his father was making a mistake and tried to put Jacob's right hand on the head of Manasseh. Jacob was a prophet and knew by the Holy Spirit that Ephraim would be the more important, and so he put Ephraim before Manasseh, 48.17-22. Jacob was sure that God would bring his family back to Canaan as He had promised, so he gave Joseph a special piece of land.

It is natural that the older son should have the chief place, but in this chapter, Joseph was given the chief place instead of Reuben, and Ephraim instead of Manasseh. Neither Ishmael nor

Esau got the blessing of the firstborn. Amnon was the oldest son of David, 2 Samuel 3.2, but Solomon became king when David died. This is always God's way; spiritual things are more important than what is only natural.

Jacob blessed his twelve sons, chapter 49

6/24   Jacob had not been a perfect saint with God in his early days and he had to reap what he had sown. However he learned the lessons which God gave him and his name was changed to Israel. He had to say that he had had a hard time, 47.9, but at the end of his life he could say that God had led him all the way and delivered him from all evil, 48.15,16. He was also a prophet of God and he could now give in chapter 49 a blessing to each of his twelve sons and tell them something of their future.

Reuben, 49.3,4

Reuben was Jacob's oldest son and had many good qualities. However he had fallen into sin, 35.22, and Jacob could not trust him, 42.37,38. Reuben was like water and Jacob knew that his descendants would not become a great tribe in Israel.

Simeon and Levi, 49.5-7

Jacob remembered the cruel anger of Simeon and Levi when they went together and destroyed the men of Shechem, 34.25. Jacob saw that these two brothers would be divided. Moses and Aaron were born in the tribe of Levi and God set the Levites apart as the priestly tribe. The other tribes all received a share in the land when the nation of Israel entered Canaan. The tribe of Levi did not get any land but they received other privileges.

Judah, 49.8-12

6/25   Judah got the chief blessing; he became the ancestor of David and of our Lord Jesus Christ. Judah had fallen into terrible sin but he was fully restored to the Lord by grace. He had become surety for Benjamin when the brothers took him to Egypt. The word Judah means *praise*, and Jacob said to Judah, *Your brothers shall praise you.* They would also bow down to him, 49.8. Judah was like a lion, the king of animals, 49.9, and he would have the king's rod until finally Christ will come to rule as King of kings. Then the peoples of the world will come to obey Christ and this will bring great joy to the Lord Jesus. Wine in verses 11 and 12 speaks of this joy.

Zebulun and Issachar, 49.13-15

6/26   Jacob first blessed the first four sons of Leah, then spoke about her two younger sons. First he blessed Zebulun, the youngest of the six. Later the nation of Israel entered the land of Canaan and Zebulun and Issachar were given a place in the north between the Mediterranean Sea and the Sea of Galilee. Jacob knew that Issachar would choose the soft life and would become a slave rather than fight his enemies.

Dan, 49.16-18

Next Jacob spoke about the sons of Bilhah and Zilpah. Dan means *judging*, and Jacob prophesied that he would judge the people but not in a righteous way. In Judges 18 we read of a terrible sin of the tribe of Dan. The people of Israel often went into terrible sin, but there were always some who wanted to follow the Lord. In verse 18 Jacob spoke of these who wait for Jehovah's salvation.

Gad, Asher, Naphtali, 49.19-21

Jacob prophesied that Gad would have enemies but he would gain the victory at last. Jacob also gave short promises of blessing to Asher and Naphtali.

Joseph, 49.22-26

6/27   Jacob gave the blessing of the firstborn to Joseph, 1 Chronicles 5.1.
Joseph was like the branches of a fruit tree which ran over the wall. The family can eat the fruit of a tree planted in their own garden, but if the branches grow over the wall people outside can eat as well. So Joseph provided food for his own family and much more for the people of Egypt.

Joseph's brothers had been like men shooting arrows at him but Joseph got strength from God, 49.23,24. God would bless Joseph with all blessing, 49.25,26, because he had not gone into sin with his brothers.

Benjamin, 49.27

Benjamin would be like a wild animal fighting against his enemies and would gain the victory. Benjamin means "son of the right hand." Joseph was a picture of the Lord Jesus bringing blessing to many, but Benjamin is a picture of the Lord in judgment. This judgment will be necessary before the Lord can rule in this world in righteousness, read Psalm 110.1.

6/28 So Jacob finished blessing all his sons and commanded them again
to bury him in Canaan. Abraham and Isaac were buried in the field
of Machpelah, also Sarah, Rebekah and Leah. This was near the city of
Hebron which became very important in the days of Joshua and David.
Soon after this Jacob died, 49.28-33.

The last years of Joseph's life, chapter 50

6/29 When Jacob died, Joseph wept over his father and told his men to
prepare the body so they could bury it months later in Canaan. The
Egyptians wept for Jacob for seventy days, 50.1-3.

Joseph asked Pharaoh if he could go to the land of Canaan to bury
his father, and many of the leaders of Egypt went with him, as well as
Joseph's own family. The people of Canaan saw all these Egyptians who
had come to mourn for Jacob. Joseph and his brothers buried Jacob in
the field of Machpelah, then returned to Egypt, 50.4-14.

6/30 Soon Joseph's brothers became afraid that he would be angry with
them. They could not believe that he had really forgiven them for
all the wrong they had done to him, 50.15-21. This made Joseph very
sad, and he told them again that he had forgiven them and would continue to look after them. Joseph knew that God had forgiven him and that
he should forgive his brothers. God had control over everything and had
planned that Joseph would save many lives in the time of famine.

God has promised to forgive us through the Lord Jesus
Christ, and it makes Him sad when people will not believe this.
Many people keep on working to save themselves, and others
feel that they might be lost after all. We should just take God at
His word and believe what the Bible says, *We have been put
right with God through faith and we have peace with God
through our Lord Jesus Christ,* Romans 5.1. We should also be
ready to forgive one another. If we do not forgive our brothers,
the Father will make us pay up, Matthew 18.23-35.

Joseph himself lived to be 110 years old, 50.22-26. Before he died he
told his brothers to bury him in the land of Canaan. Joseph believed that
God would take the nation of Israel back to the land he had promised to
them, Hebrews 11.22. When Joseph died his body was kept in Egypt for
many years, then God fulfilled His promise and the people of Israel went
back to the land of Canaan.

Joseph and his brothers mourned and wept when Jacob died. It is only natural that we should feel sorry when our loved ones go, but if they are true Christians we do not feel as sorry as other people do because we know that they have gone home to be with the Lord and this is far better, 1 Thessalonians 4.13; Philippians 1.23. Joseph did not have the hope which we have, but he believed God's promise that the nation of Israel would return to Canaan.

Now test yourself

1. How many people went with Jacob into Egypt? *74 (Acts) → 66 from Jacobs descendants (Genesis)*
2. Why did Jacob give the chief blessing to his younger grandson? *He was a prophet and knew God would bless Ephraim more than*
3. Which of Jacob's sons was the greatest, Levi, Judah or Joseph? *Manoseh.*
4. Which of Jacob's sons is a picture of Christ coming to judge His enemies? *Benjamin.*
5. Where were Jacob and Joseph buried? *Canaan. (Joseph's body was buried there years later when they returned).*
6. Why did Joseph weep in chapter 50? *Wept when father died & also when brothers thought he would punish them.*

Turn to page 117 to check your answers.

All important : ① Levi (NB in Moses/Aarons time)
② Judah (Jesus' line).
③ Joseph (greatest while Jacob was alive).

-12-
The Teaching of Genesis

Genesis starts out, *In the beginning God*. The last verse ends with a dead man in Egypt. In between these two verses we have a wonderful history:

1. God created the world and man.

2. The first man fell into sin and passed on a sinful nature to all other men.

3. God judged the sin of men by bringing in the flood and saving only eight people.

4. Still man's evil heart was unchanged.

5. God in grace called out Abraham to start a new order.

6. Abraham, Isaac, Jacob and Joseph all had their own problems. Sometimes they sinned and sometimes they gained the victory.

7. God promised again and again that He would raise up a Savior for men.

In this lesson we will think of what the book of Genesis teaches about God and His creatures. You must study the whole Bible to know the truth fully. You must consider every verse on any subject to know the whole truth about that subject. No verse in the Bible denies what any other verse says, but you should not take one verse and say that it teaches something by itself. Our teaching must be according to the whole truth of God, and we need the light of all Scripture on any subject before we can say, "This is what the Bible says."

In this lesson we cannot take up everything the Bible says on each subject. We will only say what Genesis teaches about God, about Christ, and about our salvation. Here is how you do it.

Take a card or a piece of paper and cover the whole page except the part you are reading. Move the card down slowly a little at a time so you can read some more. After Frame 1 you will see a question. Think about this question and try to answer it. Then move your card down until you can read the answer. If you got the right answer, go on to the next paragraph. If your answer was wrong, go back and read again the whole paragraph, and then try again.

WHAT DOES GENESIS TEACH ABOUT GOD?

FRAME 1

The book of Genesis teaches us that there is a God and the whole Bible does the same. The Bible does not try to prove that there is a God. Some people say there is no God and would demand that we prove there is a God. The writers of the Bible do not try to argue or *prove* that there is a God.

Which of these statements is true?

1. Genesis proves that there is a God.
2. Genesis teaches that there is a God. ✓

Genesis certainly teaches that there is a God and so does the whole Bible, but the Bible does not try to argue or prove that He exists. Answer 2 is better than 1.

FRAME 2

The Bible simply starts out wonderfully with these words, "In the beginning God." From these words we learn that God had no beginning. He always was and always will be. He is *eternal.*

What did Abraham call the Lord in 21.33? *The Lord, the God who lives forever.* ✓

The Everlasting God; this is the same as calling Him eternal.

FRAME 3

The first verse in the Bible also proves that God is *supreme*, He is over all because He created everything.

What did Melchizedek call God, 14.19? *God most High* ✓

Melchizedek called God the Most High, the Supreme One.

FRAME 4

We also see that God is supreme because He has authority over man. He could tell Adam and Eve which trees in the garden they could use for food, 2.16,17. He called Abraham to leave his country, 12.1. We see that God controls the affairs of men in the story of Joseph, who became ruler in Egypt at exactly the right time, 45.8.

God is also *all powerful*. He could create the world out of nothing and man out of dust. He said to Sarah, *Is anything too hard for the Lord?* 18.14.

God Almighty ✓

What is God called in 17.1; 28.3 and 35.11?

God is called the Almighty in these verses. Also in 43.14, 48.3, 49.25. This means that God has great power and also that He takes care of those whom He loves.

FRAME 5

Genesis teaches us another thing about God: He can *know everything*. Hagar was right when she called God *the God who sees*, 16.13. God knows people's thoughts.

Why did Sarah try to lie to God, 18.12-15?

She was afraid that God would be angry with her so she tried to conceal her thoughts, but of course God knew what she was thinking. We also see that God knew what Abraham's servant was going to pray for, and Rebekah was already at the well, 24.12-15.

FRAME 6

God knows the future and He could tell Rebekah about her two sons who were not yet born.

What did God tell Joseph about the future, 37.7, 9?

God showed Joseph that his family would bow down to him. Again in chapter 49 God showed Jacob what would happen in the future.

FRAME 7

God knows the hearts of all men before they are born. He can know the future just as easily as we can know the past. For example, God chose us in Christ before the world was made, Ephesians 1.4; 1 Peter 1.2. In the book of Genesis God chose one son in a family to be the ancestor of the coming Savior. For example, God chose one of the three sons of Noah, Shem.

1. Which of Abraham's sons did God choose? *Isaac* ✓

2. Which of Abraham's grandsons did God choose? *Jacob* ✓

God chose Isaac and Jacob. Of the twelve sons of Jacob God chose Judah to be the ancestor of the Messiah, and many years later the Lord Jesus was born a descendant of these men.

FRAME 8

Here is another wonderful truth about God: God is *light*. He reveals Himself to man and we could not know anything about God if He had not revealed Himself. In Genesis we see that God revealed Himself to Adam, Eve, Cain and Noah. *Isaac* ✓

Read 12.7; 17.1; 18.1; 26.2; 35.9. To whom did God appear in these verses? *Abram (Abraham)* *Jacob* ✓

God appeared to Abraham, Isaac and Jacob. He also spoke to Abraham five times and to Jacob six times, 28.13; 31.3; 32.28; 35.1,10; 46.3. God revealed Himself and His plans through six dreams in the life of Joseph.

FRAME 9

God is supreme and all powerful, but He always acts according to His own character. He is *always the same*, He cannot lie or change. What He promises He will certainly fulfill. For example, He promised to give Abraham and Sarah a son and He did so twenty-five years later, 12.2-4; 21.5.

God also made some very strong promises or covenants with some of the men of Genesis. He made a covenant with Noah, 6.18; with Noah's descendants and all living creatures, 9.9-11; with Abraham,

15.18; 17.2; and with all his descendants, 17.7.

Name two signs of God's covenants in Genesis 9.13; 17.11.

_____Rainbow_____; Circumcision_____:

The rainbow was a sign of one of God's covenants and circumcision was another. ✓ ✓

God's great desire is to bless men, but He may have to change His mind because men are evil, 6.6. This does not mean that God's character has changed. He knew everything from the beginning and He will never change. His promise today is to bless all who trust in Christ.

FRAME 10

God is also *righteous and holy*, and we see this truth in Genesis. God had to punish sin, 2.17; 3.14-19. He sent the flood because men were so wicked, 6.6. He commanded that any murderer should be put to death, 9.5. He mixed up men's language when they disobeyed Him at Babel, 11.7.

Whom did God punish in 12.17 and in 19.26? ✓

_____King of_____ ✓ _Lot's wife_. ✓
Egypt.

God punished Pharaoh and Lot's wife. He also destroyed Sodom and Gomorrah because the people were so wicked.

We should also know that God punishes His own people. For example, Abraham was put to shame in Egypt, 12.20, and in Gerar, 20.9. You have learned that Jacob sowed deception and reaped more than he sowed. No wonder Abraham could say that the Judge of all the earth will always do what is just, 18.25.

FRAME 11

But God always shows His love and grace along with His righteousness. For example, He had to punish Adam and Eve but He gave them coats of skin, 3.21. He decided to destroy the earth with a flood but He saved Noah and his family, 6.8.

How did God show mercy and grace to Lot? Saved them ✓
_____when destroyed Sodam +_____
                        Gomorrah.

God showed mercy to Lot and his family and saved them when He sent angels to destroy Sodom and Gomorrah, 19.16.

We can see God's grace when He showed Abraham an animal which died instead of Isaac, 22.13. Even when a man is in sin, God will show grace if he repents. For example, Judah repented of his great sin and God chose him for the chief blessing.

Just where sin increases there the grace of God increases much more, Romans 5.20.

FRAME 12

The Bible everywhere teaches that there in only one God, Deuteronomy 6.4; 1 Timothy 2.5. But the New Testament adds this, that the Father, Son and Holy Spirit are equally God. This is called the teaching of the Trinity.

Sometimes you might think that there is more than one God. For example, "Let *us* make man in *our* image and likeness," 1.26; "Let *us* go down," 11.7. We cannot say that the Old Testament teaches the truth of the Trinity, but we will look at a few verses about the Father and Son and the Holy Spirit.

In Genesis 22 and 24 Abraham is a wonderful picture of God the *Father*. First he gave his son as a sacrifice, chapter 22; then he sent his servant to get a bride for his son, chapter 24.

Read 24.36; 25,5; Matthew 11.27. How has God honored His Son?
Given him all things ✓

God has glorified His Son by giving Him everything that He has, just as Abraham gave everything to Isaac.

THE SON OF GOD

FRAME 13

The Son of God was never created; He is like God, He is eternal. We know that God created the heaven and the earth.

Does the New Testament speak of the Father, the Son or the Holy Spirit in John 1.3 and Colossians 1.16? *All things made by Father (God) through Son (Jesus)* ✓

Some translations say that God created all things through Christ, but the Greek Testament says all things were made by Him, the Son of God.

FRAME 14

No one has ever seen God. The only Son has made Him known, John
1.18. The Old Testament says God appeared to man and this is really the
Son of God. The Angel of Jehovah may be considered the Son of God.
The word angel means *messenger*, and in Genesis the Angel of Jehovah
often spoke as God Himself. The Angel of Jehovah spoke to Hagar,
16.7-13; 21.17-19. The Son of God was going to be rejected by His people and He could understand the feelings of this servant woman who had
been put out.

Why would the Angel of the Lord be especially interested when
Abraham offered his son and when the servant went to get a bride for
Isaac, 22.1; 24.7? *Jesus would later be sacrifice & get
bride (church).*

The Son of God would later be offered as a sacrifice and get a Bride.

FRAME 15

Later the Son of God was to become a Man, the Savior of the world.
In Genesis 3.15 we have the first promise of the coming Deliverer.

What kind of a Savior would come? Choose the right answer.

    (a) an angel
    (b) a man
    (c) an animal

The coming Savior would be a Man. The Bible says that God
Himself would be the Savior. So God became Man, and the great
Deliverer is the God-Man.

FRAME 16

Isaac yielded to his father and obeyed him even when he thought he
would die. Here is a picture of the Lord Jesus Christ in His death.

Many animals died as sacrifices in the book of Genesis: 4.4; 8.20;
15.9; 22.13; 31.54; 46.1. Whom are these animals a picture of?
Jesus Christ   Altar = cross .

Every animal sacrifice pointed forward to the death of Christ, and
every altar pointed forward to the cross of Christ, 12.8; 13.4,18; 26.25;
33.20; 35.7. Joseph in a pit, 37.24, or in prison, 39.20, was in the place

of death and so he was a picture of Christ.

FRAME 17

The Lord Jesus Christ died and then rose again. Abraham offered his son and received him back again, Hebrews 11.19, so Isaac is a picture of Christ when *He* rose from death. Joseph was brought out of prison and received great glory; he was a picture of our Lord Jesus Christ in resurrection and glory.

The twelfth son of Jacob was given two names. How was he a picture of Christ? (Look back to page 71 if you have forgotten.)

Ben-Oni (Son of my sorrow) = *Benjamin (Son of Rht hand)* *Jesus sat at right hand of father.*

His first name Ben-oni means *son of my sorrow*; his second name Benjamin means the *son of the right hand*, 35.18. In Psalm 110.1 we see Christ at God's right hand.

FRAME 18

Now read Genesis 14.18; 24.63; 45.15; 49.9,10.

1. Who is a picture of Christ, our Great High Priest? Hebrews 6.20 *Melchizedek* ·
2. Who is a picture of Christ, coming to meet His Bride? 1 Thessalonians 4.17 *Isaac* ·
3. Who is a picture of Christ, finally accepted by His brothers? Romans 11.26 *Joseph* ·
4. Who is a picture of Christ winning the victory and overcoming as a lion? Revelation 5.5 *Judah* ·

---

1. Melchizedek
2. Isaac
3. Joseph
4. Judah

THE HOLY SPIRIT

FRAME 19

We read about the Holy Spirit only three times in Genesis. Notice His work:

1. In Creation, 1.2; Job 33.4.

2. With sinners, 6.3.

3. In the believer, 41.38.

Now read John 14.17; 16.8,13.

1. Which of these verses teaches that it is the work of the Holy Spirit to show sinners their sinfulness and the need of salvation? *John 16:8*

2. Which of these verses show that He lives in the believer? *John 14.17*

He works with sinners as He did with the wicked men before the flood, John 16.8.

The Holy Spirit worked through people like Joseph in Old Testament times, Genesis 41.38, but in New Testament times He lives forever in every believer, John 14.17.

We can also see a picture of the Holy Spirit in the servant of chapter 24, who was sent forth by the father to get a bride for the son. The servant gave gifts to the bride, 24.22,53, and the Holy Spirit gives gifts to the Church, 1 Corinthians 12.4-11.

ANGELS

FRAME 20

Angels are spirits created by the Son of God, Colossians 1.16, to do God's will. God put angels at the east of the Garden of Eden to guard the way to the tree of life, 3.24.

Read 19.1 and 32.1. Whom did angels come to help in these verses? *Lot ✓   Jacob ✓*

They came to deliver Lot and his family before they destroyed Sodom and Gomorrah, 19.1. They came to help Jacob when he was afraid of his brother Esau, 32.1.

FRAME 21

We know that some angels followed Satan and refused to obey God. It may be that some of these began to mix with men, 6.2. Satan was the greatest of the fallen angels, and we can surely see him coming in the form of a serpent to tempt Eve.

Satan raised a question or doubt and told a lie, 3.4,5. Which came first?   *daubt then lie* ✓

First Satan raised a doubt in Eve's mind and then he told a straight lie. This is his usual method.

FRAME 22

Who is the Descendant of the woman and how will Satan be overcome, 3.15? (Look at your book if you have forgotten.)

The Lord Jesus Christ is the Descendant of the woman and He had to die to overcome Satan.

Satan is always fighting against God's plan. In Genesis Satan tried to destroy the early ancestors of the Lord Jesus or lead them into sin. But God kept His people through every danger and we can be sure that He always will.

MAN

FRAME 23

In Genesis we learn that God created man in His own image. God is Spirit, but man is body, soul and spirit, 1 Thessalonians 5.23.

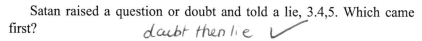

Read 45.27; 47.18; 49.6, and write down which verse speaks of man's spirit, soul and body.

Genesis 45.27 speaks of Jacob's *spirit*; 47.18 speaks of the *bodies* of the men of Egypt; 49.6 refers to Jacob's *soul*. Man is superior to all animals because he has a spirit. Adam gave a name to every living creature, 2.19.

FRAME 24

Man fell into sin and therefore he has to die; his spirit and soul leave his body. At first the people of God lived to very great ages but still this sinful nature was passed on from father to son. At the end of Genesis men did not live much longer than people do today.

What is a good old age according to Psalm 90.10?   *70 - 80* ✓

Seventy years is a good life but some people can live until they are eighty.

SIN

FRAME 25

In Genesis we learn how sin entered, and some of its terrible results. Cain knew that his father had refused to obey God's command and Cain also understood the results of that sin. Still he tried to come to God with his own sacrifice, not the kind of sacrifice which God had chosen.

Next Cain murdered his brother and refused to repent. Most of Adam's descendants followed the way of Cain and God saw that man's thoughts were only and always evil, 6.5. God showed that He hates sin by sending the flood which destroyed most men.

Four men came out of the ark and two of them fell into sin. Write down the names of these two men, Genesis 9.   *Noah + Ham .* ✓

Genesis 9.21,22 show that both Noah and his son Ham fell into sin.

SALVATION

FRAME 26

We have also many beautiful pictures of our salvation in Genesis. Many animals were sacrificed and all of them are pictures of Christ who died for us. Judah offered to be a surety for Benjamin and so he became a picture of the Lord Jesus who was willing to pay our debt, 43.9.

By dying the Lord Jesus has made it possible for men to be saved, but we need to have faith in order to get salvation. Abraham is a great example of faith in Genesis, but there are others also.

You know Hebrews 11 is a great chapter because it tells us about many people who had faith. Find the names of seven people in Hebrews

11.4-22 whose names you have read in Genesis.

Abel, Enoch, Noah, Sarah, Isaac, Jacob and Joseph are all listed in Hebrews 11 because they acted by faith.

FRAME 27

We are not only saved from sin when we believe, we are also *reconciled* to God. This means God has changed us from enemies into His friends, 2 Corinthians 5.18. We are no longer afraid of God; instead we start to love Him.

Would you say that Cain was reconciled to God, 4.6-16?

--- *NO* ✓ ---

No, Cain went away from the Lord and never showed any sign of loving God.

FRAME 28

Joseph's brothers were slow to believe that Joseph would really forgive them, 45.5,15, and later began to wonder again about it, 50.15-21.

Many people today just can't believe that God would really forgive them through faith. They say they believe but are still afraid that God might reject them in the end.

FRAME 29

When a man is saved God gives him *victory* over sin. Tell of one case of a man of God in Genesis who gained the victory over sin.

--- *Joseph* ✓ ---

Joseph is a great example of a man who overcame great temptation and gained the victory, 39.8. We should remember that God always gives us enough power to overcome temptation, 1 Corinthians 10.13.

FRAME 30

A person has to be truly born again before he can really *worship* God. Read Genesis 5.22; 6.9; 22.5; Hebrews 11.21, and name two men who worshiped God and two men who walked with Him.

Enoch and Noah walked with God. Abraham and Jacob worshiped Him.

THE BIBLE

FRAME 31

God gave us the Bible, and it is God's Word for men today. In the book of Genesis we see that God spoke to men and they wrote down the record of how God dealt with them; they did not want their children to forget God's promises. These writings were later included with Exodus, Leviticus, Numbers and Deuteronomy, which were called the books of Moses, Luke 24.27,44.

How did the Lord Jesus show that Abraham, Isaac and Jacob were real people of God, Matthew 22.32?

The Lord Jesus called God the God of Abraham and the God of Isaac and the God of Jacob. He would not have said these words unless the book of Genesis is true.

THE CHURCH

FRAME 32

The New Testament gives us the truth about the Church, but in the Old Testament we can see pictures of it. God formed Eve as a partner for Adam, 2.18. Adam in deep sleep was a picture of Christ when He died. After this Adam took Eve as his bride so we see Eve was a picture of the Church.

The servant brought Rebekah from a distant country to be with Isaac. She is a picture of the Church which the Holy Spirit is taking out of this world to present to Christ.

When did Joseph get his bride?

After he received great glory in Egypt. In the same way Christ has entered into glory, and He will soon receive the Church as His bride.

FUTURE THINGS

FRAME 33

In Genesis there are pictures of the future, but other parts of the

Bible tell us what God is going to do in this world in days to come. We know that many believers will not die, they will be caught up to meet the Lord in the air, 1 Thessalonians 4.17. After that the Lord Jesus will come and rule as King over the whole earth for a thousand years.

Read Genesis 5.24; 41.44,45; and Hebrews 11.5.

Who is a picture of the Church when the Lord takes it to heaven?

Who is a picture of Christ when He rules over the world?

Enoch is a picture of the Church, and Joseph is a picture of Christ as King.

The Lord Jesus will rule for a thousand years and then God will create a new heaven and a new earth, Revelation 21.1. These will last for ever, for all eternity. God always was God in the eternal ages of the past. He will be God for ever in the eternity of the future.

The history of man begins in Genesis when God created the heavens and the earth. Genesis tells us the beginning of everything, but does not tell us the end of anything. The rest of the Bible tells us more about God and His wonderful ways. Believers will live with God for ever, for eternity. Even now it is our joy to know the eternal God:

From everlasting to everlasting Thou art God

Psalm 90.2

APPENDIX

Genesis and Evolution

In many schools people are taught to believe in Evolution. This theory says that every living thing has developed naturally from a simple form. There were several steps.

1. The salt in the ocean changed form and some of it became a living cell. This was very small but it was able to grow and produce other cells of the same kind.

2. Some of these cells began to change a little and combined with each other so that other forms of life appeared. After millions of years there were fish.

3. Some fish crawled up on the land and gradually became birds or animals such as the horse or the monkey.

4. After many millions of years monkeys gradually changed into men. All this was just by chance.

This theory of evolution is hard to prove but many people believe in it because it leaves God out. It does not explain who created the earth in the first place, or who planned it so that all living things developed in such a wonderful way.

The Bible says God created the world out of nothing, so it is not so hard to believe that He created living things and all their various forms.

Man is not just a monkey with a bigger brain. Man has a spirit and God created him that way. We can know God, worship God, and we are responsible to obey Him. The Bible teaches that He is a God of love but also a holy God. Let us learn to obey Him because He is holy and worship Him because He is love.

HERE ARE THE ANSWERS:

Page 11

1. Only the Creator can tell and He has done so in the Bible.

2. God created the world perfect but it became dark and without form as seen in Genesis 1.2.

3. Verses 1, 21, 27. (It is found again in 2.4; 5.1,2; 6.7.)

4. Man has a three-part nature and God exists as Father, Son and Holy Spirit.

5. The Bible does not say that the work of the second day was good, but this does not mean that it was bad.

6. In the New Testament, but there are pictures of the Church in the Old Testament; for example, Adam and Eve remind us about Christ and the Church.

Page 17

1. Eve said God told Adam not to *touch* the fruit of the tree of knowledge of good and evil. Then Satan quickly told the second lie; he said that they would not die.

2. She thought she would be like God if she knew good and evil.

3. "The woman gave me the fruit." Adam also blamed God by saying, "The woman *you* gave me."

4. He promised that Eve's Descendant would win the victory over Satan. He gave both of them the skin of an animal for clothing.

5. He was separated from God the very day he sinned but he lived on earth for many years, Genesis 5.5.

6. Yes, He spoke to him after he brought the wrong offering, 4.7, and put a mark on him so he could live even though he had murdered his brother, 4.15. But Cain never repented.

Page 27

1. Enoch did not die; God took him to heaven, 5.24; Hebrews 11.5.

2 (i) God would send something when Methuselah died.

   (ii) The Lord would come with His angels to judge wicked men.

3. He is called a preacher of righteousness in 2 Peter 2.5.

4. (i) Noah walked with God and pleased God; so did the Lord Jesus.

   (ii) The ark saved men from God's judgment and Christ does the same.

5. Because they were all ancestors of our Lord Jesus Christ.

6. God wanted men to spread out over the earth, not to build cities, so He judged men by mixing up their language so they would not be able to understand one another.

Page 36

1. The journey to Canaan. God told Abraham to go to Canaan. First he stopped in Haran, then he went on to Egypt. Neither of these journeys was in the will of God.

2. It was a good place for cattle and Lot thought it looked like the Garden of Eden or the land of Egypt, 13.10.

3. Melchizedek was both priest and king. He was priest of the Most High God and he was king of peace and righteousness.

4. God promised that Abraham's descendants would be like the stars of heaven, 15.5,6.

5. God had promised that Abraham would have a son, but Abraham did not want to wait until God's time should come. Sarai gave Hagar to Abraham and he accepted her.

6. An unconditional covenant is God's promise that He will do something for His people. It does not depend on whether they obey or not. For example, God made an unconditional covenant with Abraham in Genesis 17.

Page 44

1. Abraham, 2 Chronicles 20.7; Isaiah 41.8; James 2.23. The Lord Jesus calls His disciples His friends, John 15.15.

2. Abraham really wanted the Lord to save Lot and his family and this part of his prayer was answered.

3. No, no one turned to the Lord and even his sons-in-law would not believe him, 19.14.

4. Moab and Ben-Ammi. Lot became drunk and fell into terrible sin with his own daughters, so the children were Lot's children and also his grandchildren.

5. In Egypt he was afraid and told a lie about his wife, Genesis 12.11-13. Later he did the same thing in the country of the Philistines, 20.2.

   If you fall into sin, ask the Lord at once to forgive you and to keep you from doing the same thing again.

6. The Most High God, 14.18,19. El-Shaddai or God Almighty, 17.1. The everlasting God, 21.33. You can look back in the book if you are not sure what these names mean.

Page 52

1. It was a picture of God later offering up His Son as a sacrifice for our sins.

2. He believed that God could raise him again from the dead, Hebrews 11.19.

3. God's Son, page 48.

4. God promised the whole land to Abraham, but it was right that he should pay money to those who were living there at that time.

5. He asked the Lord to lead him to the girl whom God had chosen to be the wife of Isaac.

6. Abraham is a picture of the Father. Isaac is a picture of the Son. The servant is a picture of the Holy Spirit.

Page 59

1. Isaac and Jacob were men of faith who trusted in God. Ishmael was the son of Abraham, and Esau the son of Isaac, but they had no desire for spiritual things.

2. Isaac prayed that his wife would have a baby and Rebekah asked the Lord why she felt as she did, 25.21,22.

3. We learn this in Galatians 3.8,16.

4. God told Abraham to walk through the land, 13.17, so he lived in tents with Isaac and Jacob and God provided for all their needs.

5. None of them. Isaac planned to give God's blessing to Esau although he knew he should give it to Jacob. Rebekah and Jacob planned to deceive Isaac so Jacob would get the blessing. Esau was so angry that he planned to kill his brother as Cain had done.

6. Only Esau, Hebrews 12.16. See page 55.

Page 68

1. He thought it was quite right for him to take another wife, a daughter of Ishmael, 28.9.

2. He gave Jacob his daughter Leah to be his wife instead of Rachel.

3. Levi and Judah, because Moses was born in the family of Levi, and the Lord Jesus was born in the tribe of Judah. Joseph was the most important of all Jacob's sons because he became the great ruler of Egypt.

4. She thought they would bring her good luck.

5. Because he had cheated his brother and knew that Esau had wanted to kill him, 27.42.

6. Because God had promised that Esau would be Jacob's servant, 25.23; 27.29.

Page 78

1. They wanted Hamor and Shechem to think that they were friends so they could attack them by surprise and pay them back for Shechem's sin.

2. El-Shaddai, the Almighty God, 35.9-11.

3. He was at first Ben-oni, which means the *son of my sorrow*, but he was called Benjamin which makes us think of Christ at God's right hand.

4. Esau was not a man of God and his descendants were important only in this world.

5. His father loved him and God honored him, but his brothers hated him.

6. Five. The last one, Perez, is the ancestor of the Lord.

Page 90

1. He lied to his father and his sons lied to him.

2. God and Jacob loved Joseph, but his brothers hated him. So did the wicked woman in Egypt, but the king of Egypt gave him great honor. Later his brothers had to give him honor too.

3. (i) The long coat which his father gave him.

   (ii) The servant's clothing in Potiphar's house.

   (iii) The prison clothing.

4. He wanted his brothers to confess that they had done great wrong to him.

5. He was only interested in his younger brother.

6. The Lord Jesus was beloved by God His Father but His brothers hated Him. God has given the Lord Jesus great glory and His brothers will have to bow down to Him.

Page 97

1. 74, Acts 7.14; 66 of them were Jacob's descendants, Genesis 46.26.

2. Jacob was a prophet and he knew that God would bless Ephraim more than Manasseh.

3. Joseph was the greatest while Jacob was alive. The tribe of Levi was most important in the time of Moses. But the Lord Jesus was born in the tribe of Judah so this tribe is the most important.

4. Benjamin would be like a wild animal that can defeat its enemies, 49.27.

5. Jacob was buried in Canaan but Joseph's body was left in Egypt until the people of Israel returned to Canaan many years later.

6. He wept when his father died, 50.1; and he wept when his brothers thought that he would punish them. Also notice 42.24; 43.30; 45.14,15; 46.29.

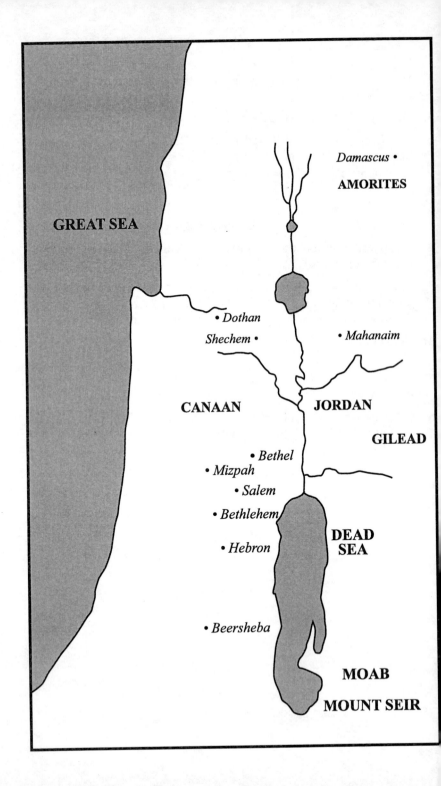